A Practice of Smart City

INTELLIGENT TAXI DISPATCH SERVICES WITH REAL-TIME TRAFFIC AND CUSTOMER INFORMATION

智慧城市的行业实践

——基于实时交通路况与用户需求的城市出租车智能调度服务

WANG HAO

汪 浩 著

北京航空航天大学出版社

内容简介

自从IBM首先提出智慧地球的理念，各国政府部门不断重视并推动相关领域的探索与研究。新加坡是智慧城市建设的先行者和实践者，其在城市智能交通领域的建设成就为世界瞩目。本书重点围绕作者在新加坡工作和学习中积累的多篇SCI/EI收录论文，以新加坡城市出租车的运营现状为背景，向读者详细展示智慧城市建设过程中，基于实时交通路况与用户需求的城市出租车智能化调度服务的研究进展与最新成果。

本书的读者对象为智能交通与物联网技术相关研究人员，高校物流专业、交通工程专业教师和研究生。

图书在版编目(CIP)数据

智慧城市的行业实践：基于实时交通路况与用户需求的城市出租车智能调度服务 = A Practice of Smart City：Intelligent Taxi Dispatch Services With Real-Time Traffic And Customer Information：英文 / 汪浩著. -- 北京：北京航空航天大学出版社，2011.4

ISBN 978-7-5124-0383-3

Ⅰ. ①智… Ⅱ. ①汪… Ⅲ. ①城市交通—出租汽车—车辆调度—研究—新加坡 Ⅳ. ①U492.4

中国版本图书馆CIP数据核字(2011)第044775号

A Practice of Smart City

INTELLIGENT TAXI DISPATCH SERVICES WITH REAL-TIME TRAFFIC AND CUSTOMER INFORMATION

智慧城市的行业实践

——基于实时交通路况与用户需求的城市出租车智能调度服务

WANG HAO

汪 浩 著

责任编辑 胡 敏

*

北京航空航天大学出版社出版发行

北京市海淀区学院路37号(邮编100191) http://www.buaapress.com.cn

发行部电话：(010)82317024 传真：(010)82328026

读者信箱：bhpress@263.net 邮购电话：(010)82316936

北京市松源印刷有限公司印装 各地书店经销

*

开本：787×960 1/16 印张：11.25 字数：252千字

2011年4月第1版 2011年4月第1次印刷 印数：1 500册

ISBN 978-7-5124-0383-3 定价：39.00元

SUMMARY

Taxis play an important role in offering personalized door-to-door service within the transport sector. Fast and efficient fleet dispatching is essential for the provision of quality customer service in a competitive taxi operation network. This book aims at developing effective dispatch strategies to improve taxi-booking services.

A satellite-based taxi dispatch system, which tracks taxis using the Global Positioning System technology for automatic vehicle location, is currently widely deployed in Singapore. Based on the booking surcharges, there are generally two categories of taxi bookings: current and advance. Current bookings are requests that taxi should reach the customer immediately or within half an hour, and advance bookings are requests made at least half an hour in advance.

The existing taxi dispatch system employed by taxi operators in Singapore to handle current bookings is based on the nearest-coordinate method, i. e. the taxi assigned for each booking is the empty one with the shortest, direct, straight-line distance to the customer location. However, the taxi assigned under this system is often not capable of reaching the customer in the shortest possible time. An alternative dispatch system has been proposed, whereby the dispatch of taxis is determined by real-time traffic conditions and the taxi assigned the booking job is the one with the shortest-time path. The effectiveness of both the existing and proposed dispatch systems was investigated through microscopic traffic simulations. This book presents and analyzes the results from a simulation model of the Singapore Central Business District (CBD) network. Results of the simulations have shown that the proposed dispatch system is capable of being more efficient in dispatching taxis more quickly; leading to more than 50% reductions in passenger pick up time and average travel distance.

Whilst for an advance booking demand under the existing dispatch system, the existing system broadcasts the booking information immediately to the island-wide taxi network in Singapore, involving both occupied and empty taxis. The job is assigned to the first taxi driver who bids for it. Obviously, under this dispatch system, advance bookings are handled on a case-by-case basis; and each booking demand (customer trip) is treated/assigned independently. Consequently, the taxi supply resource, in terms of occupancy time, may not be significantly utilized. Therefore, a novel trip-chaining strategy for taxi advance booking based on a customized algorithm of the Pickup and Delivery Problem with Time Window (PDPTW) problem has been proposed. The idea is to chain several bookings with demand time points which are spread out within a reasonable period of time, and with each pick-up point coinciding with or within close proximity to the previous drop-off location. Based on the simulation results, the proposed system for taxi advance bookings could reduce the taxi fleet size by up to 87.5%, in serving the same level of advance booking demands. This will not only result in a more reasonable fare structure for taxi services to encourage users to book taxis in advance and discourage last-minute requests, but also bring benefits to customers, drivers and taxi companies.

The trip-chaining strategy proposed in this study will have the potential to change the concept of the taxi booking service currently operating in Singapore. To further validate these proposals for both current and advance booking services in real life, a survey with a sample size of 600 respondents has been carried out to investigate users' responses. The opinions regarding the users' booking behavior, taxi arrival time and booking surcharge structure have been polled. More than 75.5% of the respondents who use current-booking service want or expect taxi to arrive as soon as possible. On the condition that they can plan the trips earlier, 75.3% of the respondents are willing to shift to use advance-booking service if the advance-booking fee is cheaper than the current booking fee, and 92.7% of the respondents are willing to obtain a taxi through advance booking when advance-booking service is cheaper than street hailing. The survey results have justified the value and feasibility of strategies proposed in this book.

BIOGRAPHY OF THE AUTHOR

Dr Wang Hao is currently the Associate Dean of School of Management, Ningbo Institute of Tech., ZheJiang Univ. He got his PhD degree from The Logistics Institute-Asia Pacific and Dept. of Civil Engineering of National University of Singapore. He graduated from Tsinghua University and Dalian University of Technology in China with M. Engg and B. Engg respectively. He was a senior consultant in Integrated Decision Systems Consultancy Pte Ltd (IDSC) in Singapore and its Chief Representative in Greater China area. He was also holding concurrent appointment as the General Manager at Jiangsu Topasia Logistics Consulting Co. Ltd in China. Before he joined IDSC, he has been a consultant in MAEDA consultancy Pte Ltd in Japan, and a research engineer in National University of Singapore.

Dr Wang worked in engineering logistics, intelligent transportation and operation research consultancy for many years. His areas of expertise include vehicle routing planning, fleet management, demand forecasting, large-scale microscopic traffic simulation, Supply Chain Management (SCM) and government policy for strategic logistics planning.

Dr Wang is also active in education and training of Modern Logistics & SCM. He is the certified trainer for International Purchasing & Supply Chain Management (IPSCM) Program promoted by United Nations/WTO as well as the certified trainer for National Logistics Professionals Training Program by China Federation of Logistics and Purchasing (CFLP). Dr Wang is the editor & author for IPSCM Program's supplementary teaching material in China.

CONTENTS

CHAPTER 1 INTRODUCTION ········ 1
1.1 RESEARCH BACKGROUND ········ 1
1.2 SCOPE AND OBJECTIVES ········ 2
1.3 GAP AND OPPORTUNITY ········ 3
1.3.1 Current Booking ········ 3
1.3.2 Advance Booking ········ 4
1.4 METHODOLOGY OF STUDY ········ 5
1.5 ORGANIZATION OF BOOK ········ 6
CHAPTER 2 REVIEW OF TAXI OPERATION AND RELATED RESEARCH ········ 8
2.1 CURRENT STATUS OF TAXI BOOKING AND DISPATCHING SYSTEMS IN SINGAPORE ········ 8
2.1.1 Overview of Taxi Services in Singapore ········ 8
2.1.2 GPS-Based Taxi Booking Service ········ 10
2.1.3 How the Dispatch System Works for Current Bookings ········ 10
2.1.4 How the Dispatch System Works for Advance Bookings ········ 12
2.2 MODELING URBAN TAXI SERVICES ········ 12
2.3 SHORTEST PATH PROPLEMS IN TRANSPORTATION MODELS ········ 14
2.3.1 Shortest Path Tree Problem and Algorithms ········ 15
2.3.2 Time Dependent Shortest Paths ········ 17
2.4. CLASSICAL AND MODERN HEURISTICS FOR THE VEHICLE ROUTING PROBLEM ········ 18
2.4.1 Characteristics of Vehicle Routing Problems ········ 19
2.4.2 Classical Heuristics for Vehicle Routing Problems ········ 21
2.4.3 Meta-Heuristics for Vehicle Routing Problems ········ 22
2.5 TRAFFIC SIMULATION MODERLS ········ 23
2.5.1 GETRAM/AIMSUN ········ 24

2. 5. 2 VISSIM 24
2. 5. 3 PARAMICS 25
2. 5. 4 Traffic Simulation Model Selection 26
2. 6 SUMMARY OF REVIEW 28
CHAPTER 3 DISPATCHING BASED ON REAL-TIME TRAFFIC CONDITIONS FOR TAXI CURRENT BOOKINGS 30
3. 1 INTRODUCTION 30
3. 2 METHOD OF INVESTIGATION 31
3. 2. 1 Shortcomings of the Existing System 31
3. 2. 2 Data Collection 32
3. 2. 3 The Study Network 33
3. 2. 4 API Programming 35
3. 2. 5 Simulation Runs 39
3. 3 RESULTS AND ANALYSIS 41
3. 3. 1 Variation of Demand Times 41
3. 3. 2 Variation of Demand Locations 45
3. 3. 3 Variation of Empty Taxi Rates 48
3. 4 SUMMARY 51
CHAPTER 4 TRIP-CHAINING FOR TAXI ADVANCE BOOKINGS 52
4. 1 INTRODUCTION 52
4. 2 THE EXISTING DISPATCH SYSTEM AND ITS DEFICIENCIES 53
4. 3 THE PROPOSED DISPATCH SYSTEM FOR ADVANCE BOOKINGS 54
4. 4 METHODOLOGY FOR THE PROPOSED DISPATCH SYSTEM ... 55
4. 4. 1 Paired PDPTW Models 55
4. 4. 2 Related Works in Literature 56
4. 4. 3 The Problem and Its Special Requirements 57
4. 4. 3 The Customized Two-Phase Method 59
4. 4. 5 The Study Network 62
4. 4. 6 Application Program Interface (API) Program for Traffic Simulation 62
4. 5 EXPERIMENTAL RESULTS 65

4.6　SUMMARY …… 69
CHAPTER 5　USERS' RESPONSE TOWARDS EXISTING TAXI BOOKING SERVICES …… 71
5.1　INTRODUCTION …… 71
5.2　MOTIVATION AND OBJECTIVE …… 71
5.3　CHOOSING SURVEY METHOD …… 73
5.4　SURVEY CONSTRUCTION AND FORMAT …… 73
5.5　COMMENTS ON THE SURVEY QUESTIONS …… 75
5.6　SURVEY RESULTS AND ANALYSIS …… 76
5.7　SUMMARY OF SURVEY …… 89
CHAPTER 6　CONCLUSIONS …… 90
6.1　CONCLUSIONS …… 90
6.2　RESEARCH CONTRIBUTIONS …… 91
6.3　RECOMMENDATIONS FOR FUTURE RESEARCH …… 93
REFERENCES …… 95
Appendix A: Sample Output File for Simulation Run …… 105
Appendix B: Simulation Results for Empty Taxi Rate 5% …… 108
Appendix C: Time Improvement Matrices for Various Empty Rates …… 113
Appendix D: Randomly Generated Demand Sets …… 115
Appendix E: Details of the Routing Solutions …… 131
Appendix F: Survey Questionnaire …… 142
Appendix G: Data of Respondents …… 145
Appendix H: Abstract of Recent Research Accomplishments …… 166

CHAPTER 1
INTRODUCTION

Taxis play an important role in offering personalized door-to-door service within the transport sector. The convenience of a comfortable and direct transportation service provided by taxis is of which mass rail transit (MRT) or buses cannot compete with. Over the years, the demand of taxi as a mode of transport has increased substantially in many cities in Asia. In Singapore, the number of trips (person trip) taken by taxi is as high as almost one million every day, which is comparable to the number of trips taken by MRT (LTA Report 2002). Meanwhile in some other metropolitan cities like Hong Kong, taxis currently form about 25% of the traffic stream in the urban area. In some critical locations, taxis form as much as 50% to 60% of the traffic stream (Transport Department 1986-2000). Evidently, taxis make considerable demand on limited road space and contribute significantly to traffic congestion even when empty (cruising to look for customers). Hence, optimization of the taxi fleet management and operation appears evocatively needed, which will reduce traffic congestion in urban area as well as improve the customer service.

1.1 RESEARCH BACKGROUND

As an important transportation mode, taxis can now be accessed/hired in public at designated taxi stands, through roadside hailing or utilization of taxi-booking services. Amongst these means, the best match between taxi demand and supply, with minimal empty cruising times in search of passengers can be brought about by an efficient taxi booking and a dispatch system. Moreover, even though taxis can be hailed anywhere on the street or waiting at taxi stands, it may be difficult to obtain a taxi during peak hours when the demand for taxis is high, or during shift changing periods.

A satellite-based taxi booking and dispatching system, which tracks taxis using the

Global Positioning System (GPS) technology for automatic vehicle location, is currently widely deployed in Singapore. With the aid of the real-time GPS-based dispatching system, the vacant taxis on the road network are tracked in the prevailing taxi dispatch system (Lee 1998; Cheng 2000).

Based on the booking surcharges, there are generally two categories of taxi bookings, current and advance. Current bookings are those where the customer makes bookings less than half an hour before the taxis are required to reach him or her (most current bookings require taxi companies to dispatch taxis immediately or as soon as possible), whilst, advance bookings are requests made at least half an hour in advance. For current bookings, the booking job is assigned to the taxi that has the shortest straight-line distance to the customer location, whereas for advance booking, the customer is assigned to the taxi driver who bids for the job within the shortest period of time.

With the advances of wireless communication, automatic vehicle location and geographic information system (GIS) technologies, the implementation of many new modes of taxi booking has been made taxi-booking services more convenient for customers. Consequently taxi booking has become the preferred choice for an increasing number of taxi customers, over street hailing and queuing at taxi stands, especially during peak demand period or at locations where empty taxis are hard to access. With the growing emphasis on customer satisfaction, it is essential for taxi operators to constantly upgrade their systems and facilities to ensure high quality services.

1.2 SCOPE AND OBJECTIVES

Traditionally, many economists have examined the models and economics of urban taxi services under various types of regulation, such as entry restriction and price control in an aggregate way. Recently, urban taxi services were modeled in a network context. At the same time, realistic methods have been proposed to describe vacant and occupied taxi movements in a road network as well as taxi drivers' search behavior for customers (Yang *at el.* 2002).

In addition to those analytical modeling approaches, increasing awareness has been drawn to improve service quality in practical taxi operations. In particular, this book involves the study of the taxi dispatch system engaged to handle taxi bookings by taxi operators in Singapore, with the intention to improve taxi dispatch services considering real-time traffic and customer information. The area of interest deals with the taxi booking services only, in which the service quality of an operator can be measured via the dispatch system. Hence other forms of taxi hiring, such as through street hailing and queuing at taxi stands, are beyond the scope of this study.

The objective of this book is to propose and verify innovative strategies for GPS-based taxi booking and dispatching system. However, the technical aspects such like how GPS works will not be dealt with specifically. Instead, attention is paid at developing models for taxi fleet management, coupled with GPS and Intelligent Transportation Systems (ITS) application on taxi dispatching in Singapore.

1.3 GAP AND OPPORTUNITY

1.3.1 Current Booking

The existing dispatch procedure for current bookings is based on the nearest-coordinate method, that is, the taxi assigned the job for a particular booking is the one that is the nearest in terms of straight-line distance to the customer location. However this assigned taxi may not essentially be the taxi that is capable of reaching the customer in the shortest possible time. There have been instances when the assigned taxi happens to be just on the opposite side of the road from where the customer is located. In order to get to the customer, the taxi driver has to make a U-turn at the next available intersection where U-turning is allowed, and this intersection happens to be some distance away. A similar problem is also encountered on one-way streets, where the taxi-driver must travel a long way before turning back to reach the customer. Thus, a taxi might be very near the customer in terms of direct straight-line distance, but it has to travel a longer time-path than a taxi approaching from a longer direct distance.

Therefore, it is possible to further improve the level of service by implementing a dispatch system that will efficiently ensure a best match for each taxi booking. This means that the proposed system will be capable of locating a taxi that will be able to reach the customer within the possible shortest time for each taxi booking. It is hypothesized that a dispatch system based on real-time traffic conditions will be able to ensure that the taxi assigned the booking job is in fact the fastest taxi to be able to reach the customer, bringing a closer match between taxi supply and demand (in terms of service time), and thus increasing customer satisfaction and reliance on taxi-booking services. With a decrease in travel time to reach each booking customer, the empty cruising times of the taxis may also be reduced as well. This study is in line with Land Transport Authority's (LTA) objectives to improve taxi services to provide car-like services, through periodic evaluation of the performance of taxi operators and the usage of GPS technology to better match demand and supply (LTA 1996).

1.3.2 Advance Booking

Whilst for an advance booking demand under the existing dispatch system, the booking information is broadcasted immediately to the island-wide taxi network in Singapore, involving both occupied and empty taxis. The job is assigned to the first taxi driver who bids for it. Obviously, under this dispatch system, advance bookings are handled on a case-by-case basis; and booking demands (customer trips) are treated/assigned independently. Consequently, the taxi supply resource, in terms of occupancy time, may not be significantly utilized.

Hence, an alternative strategy for taxi advance booking might be explored, which can take the full advantage of the information available before hand, to arrange/dispatch the taxi fleet in a more systematic manner and thus to reduce operating cost. Currently in Singapore, the surcharge of an advance booking is higher than that of a current booking. If operating cost (such as the taxi vehicle resources required and the empty cruising time caused) to deal with advance booking services is decreased significantly, then the advance-booking surcharge can be reduced or even waived to encourage more users. This could potentially change the concept of the taxi booking service in Singapore, not only resulting in more reasonable fare structures for taxi services, but also bring benefits to customers, drivers and taxi companies.

1.4 METHODOLOGY OF STUDY

In this research, a hybrid analytical-simulation approach, consisting of a customized microscopic simulation model for modeling taxi fleet movements and background traffic conditions, embedded with an analytical routing decision model to provide sensible routing plans, was proposed. Hence, the objectives of this study have actually been pursued via theoretical analyses and computer simulations using realistic road networks. Although the proof of the pudding is in the eating, it is unlikely that any authority and taxi company will allow a real-life experiment without sufficient encouragement from simulation results using realistic models.

First, the analytical model was focusing on the strategies/rules to dispatch taxi under the two different booking requests, i. e., (1) to search the most suitable taxi, which can reach the customer within the shortest time possible in response to current-booking demands, (2) to efficiently generate a set of reasonable fleet routing plan with a low operating cost to meet advance-booking demands. The details will be addressed in Chapters 3 and 4.

Subsequently, simulation models were built incorporating the strategies proposed, to evaluate their performances under simulated traffic environment. Simulation modeling is an increasingly popular and effective tool for analyzing a variety of dynamic problems, which are not amenable to study by other means. Traffic problems are characterized by the interaction of many system components or entities. These problems are usually associated with complex processes, which cannot readily be described in analytical terms. Often, the behavior of each entity and the interaction of a limited number of entities may be well understood and can be reliably represented logically and mathematically. However, the complex, simultaneous interactions of many system components cannot be adequately described in mathematical or logical forms. The numerical results from simulation provide the analyst with detailed quantitative descriptions of what is likely to happen. The graphical and animated representations of the system functions can provide insights so that the analyst can gain an understanding of why the system is behaving this way. Hence, simulation modeling was used to test the strategy proposed for its usefulness in improving taxi dispatching.

Detailed reviews on state-of-the-art simulation programs are presented in Chapter 2 PARAMICS, a microscopic simulation tool that provides suitable interface for adding user-developed routines to the main simulation process was chosen for modeling taxi behaviors. Simulation runs were performed on a selected network chosen from the Central Business District (CBD) in Singapore.

Evaluations on the performance of different systems were then made based on their efficiencies in taxi dispatch services, in terms of travel times, travel distances and number of taxis required to serve the demands. For current-booking services, additional sensitivity analysis was also carried out to investigate the influence of taxi densities in the network.

To further validate these proposals for both current and advance booking services in real life, a survey with a sample size of 600 respondents was carried out to investigate users' responses. The opinions regarding the users' booking behavior, taxi arrival time and booking surcharge structure were polled, to justify the value and feasibility of strategies proposed in this book.

1.5 ORGANIZATION OF BOOK

This book consists of six chapters that are organized as follows:

A general introduction and the background, objectives, scope and methodology of this study, as well as an outline of this book are given in Chapter 1.

Chapter 2 provides an overview of previous work in modeling urban taxi service and current status of taxi booking and dispatching operations in Singapore. Related literature of shortest path approaches in transportation model, route scheduling/planning as well as the review and selection of traffic simulation models are then presented.

Subsequently, a new method of taxi dispatching system with instantaneous traffic information is proposed and evaluated in Chapter 3. The selected results derived from simulation are also described.

Following the study of taxi current bookings, an innovative dispatch strategy was proposed in Chapter 4 to improve the ad hoc' taxi advance booking services. This practical problem is defined as STAR (Singapore Taxi Advance Reservation) in this study, which is a special version of Pickup and Delivery Problem with Time Window, a well-known NP-hard routing problem. The proposed strategy for the STAR problem was then evaluated through traffic simulation in this chapter.

To further validate the strategies proposed in Chapters 3 and 4, Chapter 5 reports a survey from taxi users' viewpoint with a sample size of 600 respondents. The opinions regarding the users' booking behavior, taxi arrival time and booking surcharge structure have been polled. A comprehensive analysis of the survey results is then demonstrated, which justifies the value and feasibility of these strategies in real life.

Finally, in Chapter 6, conclusions from this study are presented. Research contributions and recommendations for future study are appended at the end.

CHAPTER 2 REVIEW OF TAXI OPERATION AND RELATED RESEARCH

In this chapter, the state-of-the-practice of taxi booking/dispatching operations in Singapore will be presented first, followed by an overview of previous work in modelling urban taxi service. Related literature in route scheduling and planning are then reviewed, where shortest path algorithms in transportation models and heuristics for vehicle routing problems are examined. Review and selection of traffic simulation models are also given in this chapter.

2.1 CURRENT STATUS OF TAXI BOOKING AND DISPATCHING SYSTEMS IN SINGAPORE

2.1.1 Overview of Taxi Services in Singapore

Taxi services first evolved in Singapore in the 1950s, in the form of pirate taxis and school taxis, operating without any proper licenses (Chin 1998). It was only in the 1960s that the government began issuing taxi licenses to individuals and companies. Comfort Transportation Pte Ltd (Comfort Taxis) was the first official taxi company launched in 1970 with aid from the government.

The taxi fleet size grew steadily with the demand over the years, and in 1980s, the use of radiophones to handle taxi bookings was implemented to reduce the empty cruising times of taxis. The taxi fleet of 10,000 was also organized into three separate companies, which are NTUC Comfort, Yellow Top and Singapore Airport Bus Service. Only 3,000 of these taxis were equipped with radiophones at that time.

By 1990, the number of taxis fitted with radiophones went up to 6,000 out of the 11,000 taxi fleet size. This fleet of 11,000 was being managed by five taxi companies, with two new companies, Singapore Commuter and SBS Taxi Service. In 1995, these two companies then merged with Singapore Airport Bus Service to form CityCab, which is one of the four main existing taxi operators. The other three companies are Comfort Taxis, Yellow Top and TIBS Taxis. In the same year, CityCab initiated a smart booking system for dial-a-cab service, using a GPS-based system for tracking and dispatching taxis to commuters. Later, all other taxi companies switched from conventional radio-based, manual booking system to this type of GPS-based dispatch system. (Lee 1998; Cheng 2000)

Currently there are approximately 18,000 taxis in Singapore, operated by the four companies. The fare structure of taxi market is deregulated, which consists of meter fare and surcharges like booking fees. Meter fare includes flag-down fare and distance rate. The flag-down fare ranges from S$2.10 to S$2.40 (US$1 is equivalent to S$1.73 in November 2003), and distance rate ranges from 10 cents per 200 to 225 meters. The booking fee ranges from S$3.00 to S$3.20 for current bookings and $5.00 to $5.20 for advanced bookings. Hence, the booking fee could be a significant part of the total taxi fare for a short trip. Relevant information about the respective companies is summarized in Table 2.1 (as in November 2003).

Table 2.1 Taxi Operators and Booking Fees in Singapore

Taxi Company	Year formed	Fleet Size	Flag-down Fare	Current Booking Fee	Advance Booking Fee	Distance Rate
Comfort Taxis	1970	11300	S$2.40	S$3.20	S$5.20	S$0.10/225m
Yellow Top	1996	1200	S$2.40	S$3.20	S$5.20	S$0.10/225m
CityCab	1995	4900	S$2.40	S$3.00	S$5.00	S$0.10/225m
TIBS Taxis	1990	1800	S$2.10	S$3.20	S$5.20	S$0.10/220m

Note: 1 US$ = 1.73 S$ in November 2003

As one of the main features in the Singapore taxi market, taxi drivers are not the vehicle owners; instead they rent vehicles from taxi companies and the average daily rent for a taxi is approximately S$90 (LianHeZaoBao 2003). Each taxi is on the road 24 hours a day, driven by 2-3 drivers in different. Based on the information from taxi companies, LTA and taxi drivers, each taxi makes 35 trips (vehicle trip) an average day and the total travel distance is around 500 km per day, including 33%-35% of empty cruising distance. As indicated by the largest taxi company in Singapore, 12%-15% of total taxi trips cater for taxi bookings, and 3%-4% of the booking volume is actually from advance-booking jobs. The average daily profit for a taxi driver is S$68. (LianHeZaoBao 2003)

2.1.2 GPS-Based Taxi Booking Service

As mentioned earlier, in 1995 CityCab became the first operator in Singapore to launch a vehicle location and taxi dispatch system. In quick successions, the other operators followed suit. This was a major improvisation in the taxi industry, as it not only meant faster booking and dispatch services, but it also allowed the taxi companies to better manage their taxi fleet in meeting customer demands.

With this new system, computerized dispatching links commuters, taxi drivers and operators by a computer server and wireless communications. Every taxi has its location updated periodically in the server. The system can find the nearest vacant taxi, and the taxi's in-vehicle display panel can tell the driver the passenger's pickup location. Once a taxi driver accepts the customer's booking request, the system can automatically telephone the customer telling him or her the taxi's license plate number through a synthesized voice message. The system also uses interactive voice responses to prompt callers to key phone buttons to book a taxi and send the commuter's particulars to the driver.

Although the core part of GPS-based taxi tracking is essentially the same, the selection and dispatch of taxis are slightly different among the different taxi companies. The following details of how the system works are based on information provided by the largest taxi company.

2.1.3 How the Dispatch System Works for Current Bookings

A frequent taxi commuter can open an account with the taxi company for free. Bookings by non-account holders are put through to a service assistant (or telephone operator). If a non-account holder has called before, his or her trip history is recorded in the customer database and the operator will ask whether he or she wants to be picked up from the same location. By registering with the taxi company, regular users will receive individual personal identification numbers (PIN) to give them a short cut into a computerized system being introduced to speed up the booking service. Those who register as regular users must provide their particulars and up to five usual pick-up locations. The information will be keyed into the computerized customer database. The regular passenger dials with the PIN followed by a set of instructions to tell' the system the pick-up locations. If the regular customer is at a location other than those listed as usual pick-up points, he or she will have to use the operator-assisted system, like other non-registered passengers.

Registered regular customers use the system by following these steps:

ⅰ. When a regular passenger calls for a taxi by phone, the automated voice system guides him or her to key in the PIN and pick-up point.

ⅱ. The call goes to the central computer server and the booking details are sent to taxis via the wireless Mobile Data Network. Then, the passenger's pick-up point will appear on in-vehicle display panels next to the dashboard in selected empty taxis.

ⅲ. Only those empty taxis in close proximity of the customer location can receive this booking information; usually the radius of the broadcasting area is about one to two kilometers based on the current empty taxi density surrounding the pickup location.

ⅳ. Interested drivers can bid for the broadcasted job by pressing a button of the in-vehicle display panel within 8-12 seconds.

ⅴ. Among all the taxis which bid for the job, the system then selects the nearest taxi based on the straight line distance that is the nearest to the passenger's pick-up point.

ⅵ. As soon as the successful taxi driver receives the confirmation from the dispatch center, the driver can proceed to the pickup location and at the same time a computerized voice message will tell the passenger the license plate number of the assigned vehicle. When all these activities are taking place, the caller is asked to hold on to the phone line until the dispatched taxi's license plate number is given to him or her.

There are some drawbacks to this system. As the system is only able to measure the distance between a taxi and the customer location on a straight lines basis, it is unable to know the actual ground distance. It is also unable to know whether the taxi is on an expressway and in which direction it is traveling. Drivers on expressways may be heading the opposite direction and hence will need to travel a longer distance to reach the customer. Under such situation, the taxi's arrival time will be delayed, and on the other hand, it is unfair to other drivers who can actually reach the customer earlier.

2.1.4 How the Dispatch System Works for Advance Bookings

As most steps of the dispatch system to process advance bookings are same as current bookings, only the differences are highlighted in this sub-section. Unlike the current-booking information which is broadcasted only within the proximity of the customer location, the advance-booking information is broadcasted immediately to the island-wide taxi network in Singapore, involving both occupied and empty taxis. The job is assigned to the first taxi driver who bids for it.

One of the most obvious shortcomings is that this dispatch system assigns each advance-booking job to a taxi on a case-by-case basis. In other words, booking demands are treated/assigned independently. However, one piece of advance-booking job usually affects a taxi's street pickup service. In fact, many taxi drivers do not like advance bookings because they are worried that they might not be able to pick more passengers on the streets once they accept an advance booking. Eventually, they might stand more revenue loss than gain. To compensate for the opportunity cost, taxi companies have raised advance-booking fees to be higher than current-booking fees. More details of the shortcomings of this system will be addressed in Chapter 4.

2.2 MODELING URBAN TAXI SERVICES

This section presents a survey of analytical modeling methods for urban taxi services, with emphasis placed on the interaction among taxi supply, customer demand and externality of service consumption on customer waiting time and taxi utilization.

The interest of economists for the analytical aspects of the taxi market can be traced back to the early sixties. In an appendix of his first provisional edition of Price Theory', Friedman (1962) included the issue of licensing taxicabs'. This problem soon attracted interest by professional economists (Lipsey and Steiner 1966; Orr 1969). A subsequent stream of papers followed the topic continually kept up to date (Douglas 1972; Beesley 1973; De Vany 1975; Shrieber 1975, 1977; Abe and Brush 1976; Manski and Wright 1976; Foerster and Gilbert 1979; Beesley and Glaister 1983; Frankena and Pautler 1986; Gailick and Sisk 1987; Rometsch and Wolfsteter 1993; Hackner and Nyberg 1995). Early works centered on the general recognition of pervasive market failures, analysis of the effect of regulation of fares and entry under alternative assumptions regarding the market structure and the organization of the service. Recent notable studies in the topic have made significant improvements in our understanding of the market mechanism (Arnott 1996, Cairns and Liston-Heyes 1996). In addition, there have been many contributions towards the study of empirical aspects of taxi regulation/deregulation around the world (Teat and Berglund 1987; Garling *et al.* 1995; Dempsey 1996; Gaunt 1996; Gaunt and Black 1996; Morrison 1997; Radbone 1998; Schaller 1999).

The economics of taxi service has been overwhelmingly examined in an aggregated manner. A highly aggregate model was originally proposed by Douglas (1972) and has been adopted by subsequent studies on the economics of taxis. It is commonly accepted that there are two principal characteristics that distinguish the taxi market from the idealized market of conventional economic analyses: the role of customer waiting time and the complex intervening relationship between users (customers) and suppliers (firms) of the taxi service.

Recently, Yang *et al.* (1998) developed an aggregate simultaneous equations model based on the Hong Kong taxi survey data. Number of taxis, taxi fare and disposable income are used as exogenous variables; while customer and taxi waiting times, taxi utilization in terms of the percentage of occupied taxis on the roads, taxi availability in terms of vacant taxi headway and customer demand are used as endogenous variables. The functional form of the structural model is generally difficult to specify and has to be built in a heuristic manner. The nonlinear simultaneous equation model developed by Yang *et al.* (1998) is found to be able to predict general outcomes of introducing new taxi policies (issue of new taxi licenses and change of taxi fare), but the accuracy of prediction for certain variables needs to be enhanced. With the same set of data, Xu *et al*. (1999) applied a neural network approach for the analysis of the complex nonlinear relationships among the above endogenous and exogenous variables.

To precisely understand the equilibrium nature of urban taxi services and assess traffic congestion due to (both vacant and occupied) taxi movements together with normal traffic, it is necessary and important to model taxi services in a network context. In this respect, Yang and Wong and their collaborators have developed a substantial stream of researches in recent years. Their works on network equilibrium modeling of urban taxi services can be found from Yang and Wong (1997, 1998), Wong *et al*. (2001), Yang *et al*. (2002).

On the whole, modeling urban taxi service under competition and regulation is an intriguing issue worthy of analytical and computational studies by economists and transportation researchers. Indeed, the taxi market is not amenable to the usual demand-supply analysis; it has been one of the typical examples for analytical study of the economic consequences of regulation and regulatory choices.

2.3 SHORTEST PATH PROPLEMS IN TRANSPORTATION MODELS

The development and implementation of the shortest path algorithms have been the most studied network optimization problem, with interesting applications in various fields such as operations research, transportation, management science and computer science. An enormous number of shortest path algorithms have been published since the end of the 1950s (Dijkstra 1959, Floyd 1962, Van 1978, Dial *et al*. 1979, Gallo and Pallottino 1984, Glover *et al*. 1985, Ahuja *et al*. 1990, Bertsekas 1991, Goldberg and Radzik 1993).

In many transportation problems, shortest path problems of different kinds need to be solved. These include both classical problems, for example to determine the shortest paths (under various measures, such as length, cost and so on) between some given origin/destination pairs in a network, and also non-standard versions, for example to compute the shortest paths either under additional constraints or on particular structured graphs.

Due to the nature of the applications, transportation scientists need very flexible and efficient shortest path algorithms, both from the computing time point of view and in terms of memory requirements. Since no best' algorithm exists for all kinds of transportation problems, i. e. no algorithm exists which shows the same practical behavior independently of the structure of the network, of its size and of the cost measure (cost function) used for evaluating the paths, research in this field has recently moved to the design and the implementation of ad hoc' shortest path procedures, which are able to capture the peculiarities of the problems under consideration.

In the first part of this section, after presenting the problem, a brief review is given to a series of the classical and recently developed shortest path algorithms, then the second part is devoted to dynamic shortest path problems.

2.3.1 Shortest Path Tree Problem and Algorithms

Let $G=(N,A)$ be a simple directed network, where N is a set of nodes and A is a set of links. Each arc $(i,j)\in A$ is assigned a cost c_{ij}, which represents the travel cost to go from nodes i to j. Given a root r, the shortest path problem consists of finding a directed tree T such that the path from r to i in T is one of the shortest paths from r to i in G. Using the linear programming notation, the problem can be formulated as follows:

$$\min \sum_{ij} c_{ij} x_{ij}$$

$$\sum_{(j,i)\in BS(i)} x_{ji} - \sum_{(i,j)\in FS(i)} x_{ij} = b_i \qquad \forall\, i \in N$$

$$x_{ij} \geqslant 0 \qquad \forall\,(i,j)\in A \tag{2.1}$$

Where $FS(i)=\{(i,j)\in A\}$ and $BS(i)=\{(j,i)\in A\}$ denote the forward star and backward star of i, respectively. If $x_{ij}=1$, then the path involves the link from nodes i to j. $x_{ij}=0$ otherwise.

The necessary and sufficient optimality condition for the shortest path tree problem may be stated as T is a shortest path tree with origin r if and only if the following condition holds:

$$d_i + c_{ij} - d_j \geqslant 0, \quad \forall (i,j) \in A \tag{2.2}$$

where, d_i denotes the distance from origin r to node i. According to Gallo and Pallottino (1984), most of shortest path algorithm can be viewed as performing the prototype labeling operations, which consecutively check and adjust the nodes whose labels do not satisfy this condition while updating the shortest path tree at the same time. Based on the exploration of complete forward stars, the general implementation procedure of the SPT algorithm is given as follows:

Step 1. Initialization: dist[r]=0, p[r]=0
dist[i]=∞, $\forall i \neq r$
$q=\{r\}$

Step 2. Scan candidate list and update: do while $q \neq \varnothing$
remove i from q
for each link $(i,j) \in FS[i]$
if dist[j]>dist[i]+c_{ij}, dist[j]=dist[i]+c_{ij} p[j]=i
if $j \notin q$ $q=q \cup \{j\}$

Where, dist[i] denotes the distance from origin r to node i. q is the candidate list. p denotes the node before node i. The different algorithms are derived from this prototype by properly selecting the operation of the candidate list q, of which the two major types are label-setting and label-correcting. In general, the label-setting algorithms checks and removes a node whose label is minimum over all other nodes in q in each iteration. The algorithm ends after n iteration when no node reenters q. The time complexity of these algorithms heavily depends on how the q is stored and how the minimum label is found. The first version of label-setting method is Dijkstra's algorithm where q is implemented as an unordered linked list. Different implementations of q had been proposed to obtain the better search efficiency, most of which employed the special data structure such as heap, bucket and their combination. Heap-type algorithms offer the logarithmic complexity of scanning q using the binary heap (Williams 1964) or Fibonacci heap (Fredman and Tarjan 1987). In the bucket-type methods, the elements of q are partitioned into a sequence of buckets of width k, which is decided by the largest link length. The famous *Dial* algorithm (Dial *et al.* 1979) is a specialized bucket-type algorithm when k equal to 1 and all link costs are integers. Moreover, combined the bucket-type algorithm with the heap structure, one may obtain very good polynomial complexity bounds. An example of radix-heap proposed has been by Ahuja *et al.* (1990). However, as suggested by Bertsekas (1998), simpler algorithms, such as *Dial*, has been more popular in practice. On the other hand, although they do not avoid the multiple entrances of nodes into q, the label-correcting algorithms cut off the manipulation time in node selection so dramatically that they often outperform their label-setting competitors, particularly when the network is sparse. Again, the data structure of q affects the number of iterations thereby deciding the computational overhead of the label-correcting algorithms. Two most used implementations of q are the queues and the stacks, which follows the first-in-first-out (FIFO) and last-in-first-out (LIFO) nodes selection order respectively. Generally, queues-type algorithm obtains polynomial complexity bound while the worst complexity time of stacks-type algorithm is exponential. However, the appropriate combination of queue and stack may result in very good practical efficiency in some cases, as shown by Pape (1974) and Pallottino (1979). Other typical algorithms can be found in the following papers (Bellman 1958; Ford and Fulkerson 1987; Moor 1957; Glover *et al.* 1985; Bertsekas 1993; Chen and Powell 1997).

2.3.2 Time Dependent Shortest Paths

Interesting problems, which frequently arise in transportation applications, are the so-called Dynamic Shortest Path Problems, where the factor 'time' is taken into consideration. Applications usually concern street networks, real-time intelligent transportation systems and so on (Pallottino and Scutella 1997, Palma *et al.* 1993, Kaufman and Smith 1993). Given a directed graph $G=(N, A)$, in a dynamic problem, a positive travel time or delay $d_{ij}(t)$ is associated with each arc (i, j) with the following meaning: if t is the (nonnegative) leaving time from node i, then $t+d_{ij}(t)$ is the arrival time at node j. In addition to the delay, a time-dependent cost $c_{ij}(t)$ is generally associated with (i, j), which is the cost of traveling from i to j through (i, j) starting at time t. Furthermore, there is the possibility of waiting at the nodes; in particular, a (unit time) waiting cost $w_i(t)$ can be associated with each node i, which gives the (unit time) cost of waiting at i and at time t.

Several models have been defined and analyzed depending on the properties of the delay and cost functions (e. g. continuous or discrete), on the possibility of waiting at the nodes (e. g. no waiting, waiting at each node, waiting only at certain nodes), and on the choice of the leaving time from the origin nodes (in particular, dynamic shortest paths for a fixed leaving time, independently of the leaving time, or for all the possible leaving times).

2.4 CLASSICAL AND MODERN HEURISTICS FOR THE VEHICLE ROUTING PROBLEM

The models and algorithms proposed for the solution of vehicle routing and scheduling problems, reviewed in this section, can be used effectively not only for the solution of problems concerning the delivery or collection of goods but for the solution of different real-world applications arising in transportation systems as well. Some applications are, for instance, solid waste collection, street cleaning, school bus routing, dial-a-ride systems, routing of sales people, and of maintenance units.

More than 40 years have elapsed since Dantzig and Ramser (1959) introduced the Vehicle Routing Problem (VRP). In their paper, the authors described a real-world application (concerning the delivery of gasoline to gas stations) and proposed the first mathematical programming formulation and algorithmic approach for the solution of the problem. A few years later, Clarke and Wright (1964) proposed an effective greedy heuristic that improved on the Dantzig-Ramser approach. Following these two seminal papers, many exact or heuristic algorithms were proposed for the optimal or approximate solution of the different versions of the VRP.

There are several main survey papers on the subject of VRP. A classification scheme was given in Desrochers *et al.* (1990). Laporte and Nobert (1987) presented an extensive survey that was entirely devoted to exact methods for the VRP, up to the late 1980s. Other surveys covering heuristic methods as well as exact algorithms, were presented by Christofides *et al.* (1979), Magnanti (1981), Bodin *et al.* (1983), Christofides (1985), Laporte (1992), Fisher (1995), Toth and Vigo (1998), and Golden *et al.* (1998). An annotated bibliography was proposed by Laporte (1997), and an extensive bibliography was presented by

Laporte and Osman (1995). A book on the subject was edited by Golden and Assad (1988).

2.4.1 Characteristics of Vehicle Routing Problems

In this section, a formal definition is given to the basic VRP problems. First, the Capacitated VRP is described, which is the simplest and most studied member of the VRP family. Then, the Distance-Constrained VRP, the VRP with Time Windows, the VRP with Backhauls, and the VRP with Pickup and Delivery are introduced.

1. Capacitated and Distance-Constrained VRP

In the basic version of the VRP, termed the Capacitated VRP (CVRP), all the customers and demands are deterministic, known in advance, and cannot be split. The vehicles are identical and based at a single depot, and only the capacity restrictions for the vehicles are imposed. The objective is to minimize the total cost (i.e., a weighted function of the number of routes and their length or travel time) to serve all the customers.

The CVRP may be described as the following graph theoretic problem. Let $G=(V, A)$ be a complete graph, where $V=\{0,\cdots,n\}$ is the vertex set and A is the arc set. Vertices $i=1,\cdots,n$ correspond to the customers, whereas vertex 0 corresponds to the depot. Sometimes the depot is associated with vertex $n+1$. A nonnegative cost, c_{ij}, is associated with each arc $(i,j)\in A$ and represents the travel cost to go from vertices i to j. Each customer $i\,(i=1,\cdots,n)$ is associated with a known nonnegative demand, d_i, to be delivered, and the depot has a fictitious demand $d_0=0$. Given a vertex set $S\subseteq V$, let $d(S)=\sum_{i\in S}d_i$ denote the total demand of the set. A set of K identical vehicles, each with capacity C, is available at the depot, where $d_i\leqslant C$ for $i=1,\cdots,n$. Each vehicle may perform at most one circuit/route, and the number of available vehicles is assumed to be sufficient to serve all the customers.

The CVRP consists of finding a collection of exactly K simple circuits (each corresponding to a vehicle route) with the minimum total cost, defined as the sum of the costs of the arcs belonging to the circuits, and such that

i. Each circuit visits the depot vertex;

ⅱ. Each customer vertex is visited by exactly one circuit;

ⅲ. The sum of the demands of the vertices visited by a circuit does not exceed the vehicle capacity, C.

The CVRP is known to be NP-hard (in the strong sense) and generalizes the well-known *Traveling Salesman Problem* (TSP). One variant is the so-called Distance-Constrained VRP (DVRP), where for each circuit the capacity constraint is replaced by a maximum length (or time) constraint. The case in which both the vehicle capacity and the maximum distance constraints are present is called Distance-Constrained CVRP (DCVRP).

2. VRP with Time Windows

The *VRP with Time Windows* (VRPTW) is the extension of the CVRP in which capacity constraints are imposed and each customer i is associated with a time interval $[a_i, b_i]$, called a *time window*. The time instant in which the vehicles leave the depot, the travel time, t_{ij}, for each arc $(i,j) \in A$ and an additional service time s_i for each customer i are also given. The service of each customer must start within the associated time window $[a_i, b_i]$, and the vehicle must stop at the customer location for s_i time period. Moreover, in case of early arrival at the location of customer i, the vehicle is normally allowed to wait until time instant a_i, i. e., until the service may start.

3. VRP with Backhauls

The VRP with Backhauls (VRPB) is the extension of the CVRP in which the customer set $V \setminus \{0\}$ is partitioned into two subsets: *n Linehaul customers*, and *m Backhaul customers*. In the VRPB, a precedence constraint between linehaul and backhaul customers exists: whenever a route serves both types of customer, all the linehaul customers must be served before any backhaul customer may be served.

4. VRP with Pickup and Delivery

In the basic version of the *VRP with Pickup and Delivery* (VRPPD), each customer i is associated with two quantities dl_i and pk_i, representing the demand of homogeneous commodities to be delivered and picked up at customer i, respectively. For each customer i, O_i denotes the vertex that is the origin of the delivery demand, and D_i denotes the vertex that is the destination of the pickup demand. It is assumed that, at each customer location, the delivery is performed before the pickup.

2.4.2 Classical Heuristics for Vehicle Routing Problems

Several families of heuristics have been proposed for the VRP. These can be broadly classified into two main classes: *classical heuristics*, developed mostly between 1960 and 1990, and *meta-heuristics*, whose growth has occurred in the last decade. Most standard construction and improvement procedures in use today belong to the first class. These methods perform a relatively limited exploration of the search space and typically produce good quality solutions within modest computing times. Moreover, most of them can be easily extended to account for the diversity of constraints encountered in real-life. Therefore, they are widely used in commercial software packages. In meta-heuristics, the emphasis is on performing a deep exploration of the most promising regions of the solution space. These methods typically combine sophisticated neighborhood search rules, memory structures, and recombination of solutions. The quality of solutions produced by these methods is higher than that obtained by classical heuristics, at expense of increased computing time. Moreover, the procedures usually are context dependent and require finely tuned parameters, which may make their extension to other situations difficult. In this sense, meta-heuristics are no more than sophisticated improvement procedures, and they can be viewed as enhancements of the classical heuristics.

Classical VRP heuristics can be broadly classified into three categories. *Constructive heuristics* gradually build a feasible solution while considering the solution cost (objectives), but they do not contain a solution improvement phase. The Clarke and Wright (1964) algorithm is perhaps the most widely known constructive heuristic for the VRP, which is based on the notion of cost savings. Secondly, in *two-phase heuristics*, the VRP problem is decomposed into its two natural components, clustering of vertices into feasible routes and actual route construction, with possible feedback loops between the two stages. Two-phase heuristics are divided into two classes: *cluster-first*, *route-second methods* and *route-first*, *cluster-second* methods. In the first case, vertices are first organized into feasible clusters, and a vehicle route is constructed for each of them. In the second case, a tour is first built on all vertices and is then segmented into feasible vehicle routes. Finally, *improvement methods* attempt to upgrade any feasible solution by performing a sequence of edge or vertex exchanges within or between vehicle routes (Toth and Vigo 2002).

2.4.3 Meta-Heuristics for Vehicle Routing Problems

In recent years several meta-heuristics have been proposed for the solutions of the VRPs. These are general solution procedures that explore the solution space to identify good solutions and often embed some of the standard route construction and improvement heuristics belonging to the classical heuristics for the VRPs. In a major departure from classical approaches, meta-heuristics allow deteriorating and even infeasible intermediary solutions in the course of the search process. The best-known meta-heuristics developed for the VRP typically identify better local optima than earlier heuristics, but they also tend to be more time consuming.

Six main types of meta-heuristic have been applied to the VRP (Gendreau *et al.* 2002): Simulated Annealing (SA), Deterministic Annealing (DA), Tabu Search (TS), Genetic Algorithms (GA), Ant Systems (AS), and Neural Networks (NN). The first three algorithms start from an initial solution x_1 and move at each iteration t from x_t to a solution x_{t+1} in the neighborhood $N(x_t)$ of x_t until a stopping condition is satisfied. If $f(x)$ denotes the cost of x, then $f(x_{t+1})$ is not necessarily less than $f(x_t)$. As a result, care must be taken to avoid cycling. GA examines at each step a population of solutions. Each population is derived from the preceding one by combining its best elements and discarding the worst. An ant system is a constructive approach in which several new solutions are created at each iteration using some of the information gathered at previous iterations. Tabu search, genetic algorithms, and ant systems are methods that record, as the search proceeds, information on solutions encountered and use it to obtain improved solutions. Neural network is a learning mechanism that gradually adjusts a set of weights until an acceptable solution is reached. The rules governing the search differ in each case, and these must also be tailored to the nature of the problem at hand. Also, a fair amount of creativity and experimentation is required.

This meta-heuristics for the VRP shows that the best of these methods can find excellent and sometimes optimal solutions to instances with a few hundred customers, albeit at a significant cost in computation time (Barr *et al*. 1995). Tabu search now emerges as the most effective approach. Procedures based on pure genetic algorithms and on neural networks are outperformed by Tabu search method, while those based on simulated or deterministic annealing and on ant systems are not quite competitive (Barbarosoglu and Ozgur 1999).

2.5 TRAFFIC SIMULATION MODERLS

Recently, simulation model has become one of the most useful and powerful tools for transportation analysis and design, by its proven ability to help the traffic engineers to find solutions for designing new transportation systems, or to evaluate the impact of the proposed changes to an existing transportation system. A recent research that assessed road transport models and system architectures has identified four main uses for simulation models in ITS (Boxill and Yu 2000):

i. Simulation models can be developed to assess a set of transportation control options off-line, because the on-street evaluation is difficult and expensive to collect enough data to produce statistically significant conclusions.

ii. Simulation models can be used when analyses are needed for immediate results, such as real-time or faster than real-time evaluation of a set of possible responses to incident.

iii. Traffic simulation can model the interaction of changing traffic flows under responsive control systems within the network.

iv. Sophisticated driving simulators are being developed to allow the assessment of many new in-car systems in a totally safe environment.

Traffic simulation models can be classified as: microscopic, macroscopic and mesoscopic models. Microscopic models predict the state of individual vehicles continuously or discretely, macroscopic models aggregate the description of traffic flow and mesoscopic models include aspects of both macro and microscopic models.

Among the numerous from of transportation related simulation models, microscopic traffic simulation models are specially suited to simulate the actual traffic conditions on road networks. This is not only because of its ability to have the full control of time dependent traffic scenario, but also being capable of dealing with driver behavior models. There are more than 50 microscopic traffic simulation models around the world, and each of them has their own advantages tailored to certain transportation applications. Based on the need of this research, the microscopic traffic simulation models which are highly applicable to this study, are introduced in the following sub-sections.

2.5.1 GETRAM/AIMSUN

Generic Environment for Traffic Analysis and Modeling (GETRAM) is an open architecture simulation model, which integrates Traffic Network Graphical Editor (TEDI), Advanced Interactive Microscopic Simulator for Urban and Non-Urban Networks (AIMSUN), and the GETRAM Extensions, an Application Programming Interface (GETRAM 2002).

The microscopic simulation model of GETRAM is mainly used for testing new traffic control systems and management policies. In addition, AIMSUN can be used for traffic state prediction and other real time applications. The main features of AIMSUN are as follows:

AIMSUN uses several driver behavior models: car following, lane changing and gap acceptance. Different traffic networks, such as urban networks, freeways, highways, ring roads, arterials and any combination of them can be handled. Simulation can be either based on input traffic flows and turning percentages, or based on O-D matrices and route selection models. AIMSUN also allows modeling different types of vehicles: cars, buses, and trucks, etc. The user may select among different headway models for vehicle generation: constant, uniform, normal, exponential, capacity and user definition through the use of the GETRAM Extensions. A variety of Route Choice models are available: fixed, binomial, multinomial logit or any other user defined model.

2.5.2 VISSIM

VISSIM is a time-stepping and behavior based microscopic traffic simulation model, developed to analyze the full range of functionally classified roadways and transit operations (VISSIM 2002). VISSIM was originally developed in the 1970s, and was commercial distributed in 1993. VISSIM can be employed as a decision support tool for traffic and transportation planners and can model: integrated roadway networks, general-purpose traffic, buses, rails, trucks, pedestrians, bicyclists, variable message signs (VMS), ramp metering, incident diversion, adaptive signal control and so on.

Furthermore, VISSIM can model 3D vehicle animation, and interface with planning/forecast models or assessment of access management strategies. VISSIM has already been applied for a variety of complex traffic tasks. Some of the typical ones are: vehicle actuated signal control strategies, fixed time controlled networks and public transport.

About the network modeling, VISSIM provides the users a graphical user interface to load a scanned layout plan of the modeled network as a background for the network editor. Besides, VISSIM is using links and connectors between links. Each link has attributes like number of lanes, gradient, free flow speed etc. Different driving habits between left-hand and right-hand driving are covered with the network model as well. It is also possible to define different distributions of desired speeds, accelerations, vehicle lengths, and passenger boarding times in VISSIM. The road infrastructure like signal heads, stop signs, yield signs, parking signs, speed signs, bus bays and tram stops are placed as particular objects allocated to links.

2.5.3 PARAMICS

PARAMICS (Quadstone 2002) is a suite of high-performance software tools for microscopic traffic simulation, including five software modules: Modeler, Processor, Analyzer, Programmer and Monitor. PARAMICS is applicable without network size limitation. In addition to the inclusion of the detailed physical description of the road network, the movement and behavior of individual vehicles are modeled in detail for the duration of their entire trip, providing accurate and dynamic information about traffic flow, travel time and congestion. Features such as bus operations, traffic signal settings, driver behavioral characteristics and vehicle kinematics are represented.

Moreover, there are three assignment methods in PARAMICS: all-or-nothing assignment, stochastic assignment and dynamic feedback assignment. All-or-nothing assignment assumes that all drivers traveling between two zones choose the same route and that link costs do not depend on flow levels. Stochastic assignment methods assume that the perceived cost of travel on each network link varies randomly, within predefined limits. Dynamic feedback assignment assumes that drivers who are familiar with the road network will re-route if information on the present state of traffic conditions is fed back to them. By taking real time information from the Paramics model, it is possible to update the routing calculations and it is also possible to run dynamic feedback together with stochastic assignment or with all-or-nothing assignments.

One of the nice features in PARAMICS is that many features of the underlying simulation model can be customized. Access is available through a functional interface, Application Programming Interface (API). This API allows additional functionality by adding more external modeling routines.

2.5.4 Traffic Simulation Model Selection

The following were the criteria established in (Boxill and Yu 2000) for evaluation of simulation models:

ⅰ. Must be capable of incorporating in the model the corresponding traffic devices such as detectors, traffic lights, Variable Message Systems, etc.

ⅱ. Must also be able to imitate the functions of traffic devices, which includes providing the specific traffic measurements at the required time intervals, increasing the phase timing in a given amount of time and implementing a traffic calming strategy.

ⅲ. Must realistically reflect driver behavior and vehicle interactions.

ⅳ. Must have the ability to model different traffic flow conditions at a higher level of detail (e. g. non-congested, congested, and incident).

ⅴ. Must simulate the variability in traffic demand in time and space, and model the growth/interaction and decay of traffic queues, as well as capacity reductions due to incidents and bottlenecks.

ⅵ. Must be capable of evaluating various control strategies.

ⅶ. Must be capable of interfacing with other control algorithms of ITS applications.

viii. Must make reliable estimates of network traffic conditions.

ix. Must predict network flow patterns over the near and medium terms in response to various contemplated information dissemination strategies.

x. Must provide routing information to guide travelers through the network.

xi. Must have the ability to model both freeway and surface street traffic.

xii. Must be well documented.

These criteria are rated based on their relative importance (as shown in Table 2.2).

Table 2.2 Rating for Evaluating Criteria

	Criteria	Important Rating
i	Model Traffic Devices	**
ii	Imitate Traffic Device Function	**
iii	Realistic Reflection of Driver Behavior and Vehicle Interaction	****
iv	High Level Modeling of Traffic Flow	****
v	Simulate Variability of Traffic Demand	****
vi	Evaluation of Control Strategies	****
vii	Interface With Other Control Algorithms of ITS Applications	****
viii	Reliable Estimates of Network Traffic Conditions	***
ix	Predict network flow patterns	****
x	Provide Routing Information to Travelers in Network	****
xi	Model both Freeway and Surface Street Traffic	****
xii	Well Documented	**

Note: Source: Boxill and Yu 2000.

Table 2.3 Summary of Models Based on Criteria

Simulation Model	AIMSUM	VISSIM	PARAMICS
Traffic devices (i)	√	√	√
Traffic device functions (ii)	√		√
Traffic calming (ii)		√	√
Driver behavior (iii)	√		√
Vehicle interaction (iii)	√	√	√
Congestion pricing (iv)			√

Table 2.3 (Continued)

Simulation Model	AIMSUM	VISSIM	PARAMICS
Incident (iv)(v)	√	√	√
Queue spillback (v)	√	√	√
Ramp metering (vi)	√	√	√
Coordinated traffic signals (vi)	√	√	√
Adaptive traffic signals (vi)	√	√	√
Interface w/other ITS algorithms (vii)	√	√	√
Network conditions (viii)	√		√
Network flow pattern predictions (ix)		√	√
Route guidance (x)			√
Integrated simulation (xi)	√	√	√
Well Documented (xii)	√	√	√
Runs on a PC	√	√	√
Graphical Network Builder	√	√	√
Graphical Presentation of Results	√	√	√

As shown in the results of evaluation (see Table 2.3), PARAMICS presents excellent abilities in modeling congested road networks and ITS infrastructures. PARAMICS can currently simulate the traffic signals, loop detectors, ramp meters, VMS and CMS signing strategies, in-vehicle network state display devices, and in-vehicle messages advising of network problems and re-routing suggestions. More available functions and suggestions in the face of ITS can be controlled through the API of PARAMICS for maximum flexibility and adaptability. Therefore, PARAMICS was applied in this study.

2.6 SUMMARY OF REVIEW

In this chapter, the current status of taxi booking/dispatching operations in Singapore was first introduced. Then, an overview of previous work in modelling urban taxi service was briefly presented.

Several techniques closely related to taxi practical operation and analytical modelling have been reviewed. These methodologies include shortest path approaches in transportation models, classical and modern heuristics for the Vehicle Routing Problem. To conduct a dynamic evaluation in which dispatching and routing strategies for individual taxi could be tested in a realistic traffic simulation environment, several traffic simulation models were reviewed in this chapter. Compared to GETRAM and VISSIM, a high performance microscopic simulation tool, PARAMICS, was selected in this study.

CHAPTER 3
DISPATCHING BASED ON REAL-TIME TRAFFIC CONDITIONS FOR TAXI CURRENT BOOKINGS

3.1 INTRODUCTION

This chapter investigates the effectiveness of the existing dispatch system based on the nearest-coordinate method in comparison to the proposed dispatch system based on real-time traffic conditions, i.e., the taxi assigned the booking will be the one with the shortest travel time as derived from the traffic conditions on the roads at the time when the booking call is received.

This was examined in an attempt to improve the dispatch system to provide a better match of a suitable taxi to each booking customer. If this study proves to be successful, then the proposed dispatch system based on real-time traffic conditions is indeed the superior system, taxi companies may consider adopting this proposed dispatch approach. With a more efficient system, service standards may be improved by reducing the waiting times of booking customers, leading to improved customer service and satisfaction.

The main objective was to evaluate the performance of the proposed dispatch system whether it is superior to the existing dispatch system in handling taxi bookings, in that it is able to assign the booking job to the most suitable taxi capable of reaching the customer within the shortest period of time. The evaluation was conducted through microscopic simulations, using the Paramics software. Simulation runs were performed on a selected network chosen from the Central Business District (CBD) in Singapore. Evaluations on the performance of both systems were then made based on their efficiencies in taxi dispatch, in terms of travel times and travel distances. A sensitivity analysis was also carried out to investigate the influence of empty taxi rates on the performance of the two systems.

3.2 METHOD OF INVESTIGATION

Research begins with the identification and analysis of the shortcomings of the existing dispatch system, followed by the collection of all the relevant information for simulation purposes. With the required data collected, the coding of network and the writing of the API program is then carried out. Upon completion, simulation runs are carried out on the study network to investigate the performance of the two dispatch systems. Results obtained from the simulation runs are then used to compare and evaluate the performance of the two dispatch systems.

Below in Figure 3.1 is a flowchart illustrating the steps of investigation adopted in this research. The steps of investigation will be elaborated in more detail in the following sections.

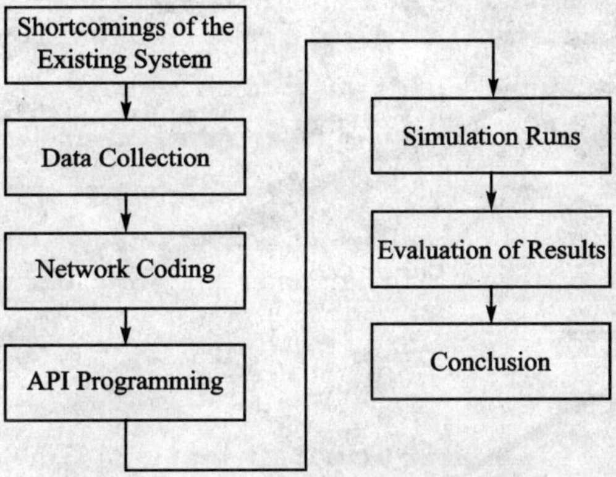

Figure 3.1 The Methodology Flowchart

3.2.1 Shortcomings of the Existing System

As introduced earlier, the existing taxi dispatch system in use by those major taxi companies, assigns a booking job to the taxi within the closest coordinate proximity to the customer, which is the taxi with the shortest straight-line distance to the customer location. However, often times, the assigned taxi may not be the fastest one to reach the customer.

Figure 3. 2 is a map of a segment of Singapore's Orchard Road. Suppose a customer at Lucky Plaza (position of cross), requests for a taxi. The taxis available are the taxis represented by the triangle and the rectangle. The current dispatch system will assign the job to the triangular taxi, as it has the shortest straight-line distance to the customer location. Although the straight-line distance of the triangular taxi to the customer location is shorter than that of the rectangular taxi, the distance the triangular taxi has to travel (see bold line) to reach the customer is longer than the rectangular taxi (see dotted line). Given similar traffic conditions on the two routes, the travel time of the triangular taxi will be longer than the rectangular taxi. Thus, if different road conditions such as one-way link, U-turn restriction and signal settings are taken into account, the disparities in travel times may be even greater.

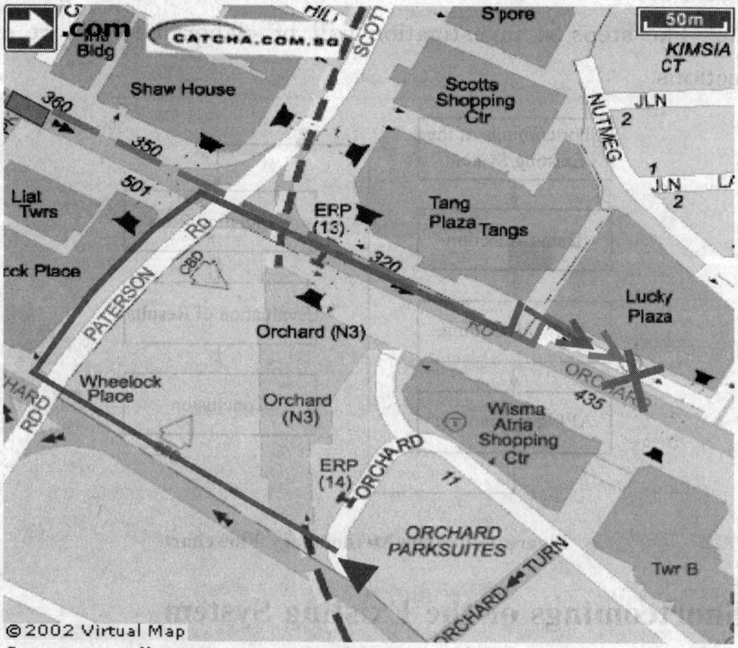

Source: streetdirectory.com

Figure 3. 2 Dispatch Routes of Taxis

3. 2. 2 Data Collection

To get started with the project, details on how the taxi operators handle each taxi booking are required for writing the Application Program Interface (API) program to simulate the current dispatch system in the Paramics environment. Hence, correspondence were made with the major taxi companies such as Comfort Transportation Pte Ltd, CityCab Pte Ltd and TIBS Taxis Pte Ltd, to find out more about their taxi booking and dispatch practices. Surveys were conducted with the taxi drivers on the roads as well, to find out more about the bidding procedure of each taxi booking.

Besides details on the current dispatch system, information on the road networks within the CBD area was also required for the coding of the CBD network. Details of the geometry and physical layout of the roads were checked up and referred to in the street directory maps (Ministry of Law 2000). The number of lanes on each road and locations of the traffic signals were also determined through appropriate road surveys.

Origin-destination (OD) statistics and information on the demarcation of zones in the CBD area were also requested from the Land Transport Authority (LTA). The OD data provided was categorized into five different vehicle types, with a separate OD matrix for each of these categories, namely taxis, cars, motorcycles, light goods vehicles and heavy goods vehicles. Green Link Determining System (GLIDE) data were also provided by LTA for the coding of signal phases and signal timings at the various intersections within the CBD region.

3.2.3 The Study Network

The network selected for this demonstration was modeled after the CBD area in Singapore, which is bounded by the Electrical Road Pricing (ERP) gantries, covering an area of approximately 3.0 km by 2.5 km.

The CBD is well serviced by a good network of roads infrastructure to serve the population commuting to and fro the CBD. It has three main arterial expressways linking commuters from the east along East Coast Parkway (ECP), from the west along Ayer Rajah Expressway (AYE) and from the north along Central Expressway (CTE) to the town center. To lower traffic congestion levels in the CBD, the Singapore government has introduced very strict controls such as the ERP Scheme, where ERP gantries are located at the borders of the CBD region to toll drivers into the CBD. Figure 3.3 shows a closer view of the CBD, with its boundary as indicated.

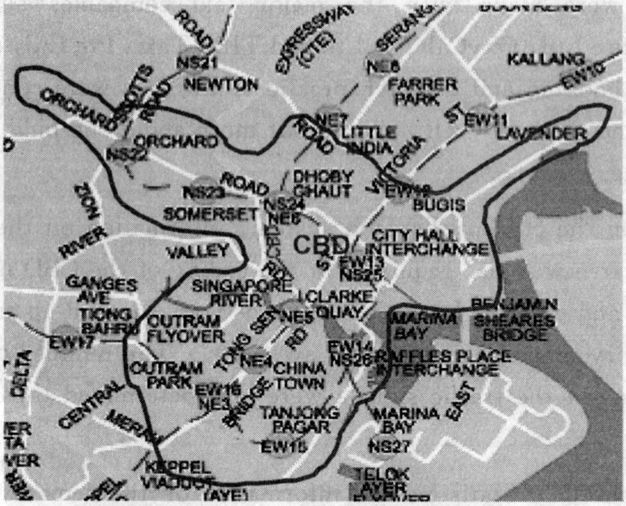

Figure 3.3 Regions bounded within the CBD

The CBD network was chosen because due to the heavy and extensive commercial and retail activities in the CBD, it is often a concentrated source of taxi bookings especially during the peak periods. More importantly, the CBD network consists of many one-way streets and few U-turning junctions, which are common features that affect the effectiveness of the current dispatch system as discussed earlier. Hence, the distinction between the performances of the two dispatch systems can be best highlighted using the CBD network.

The network of the CBD area was coded in the Paramics Modeller, adhering as closely as possible to the actual roads system, following both the layout of streets and the associated number of lanes in great detail. It consists a total of 894 nodes and 2,558 links. 100 traffic analysis zones in this network were defined as the origins and destinations of the trips made by vehicles in the network, and the traffic demand of each zone were allocated based on the real OD data provided by LTA. The 113 traffic signals at the various junctions were also coded according to the GLIDE data obtained from the LTA. On top of that, the zone data and OD information were arranged and incorporated into the network as well. Figure 3.4 provides an overview of the coded CBD road network.

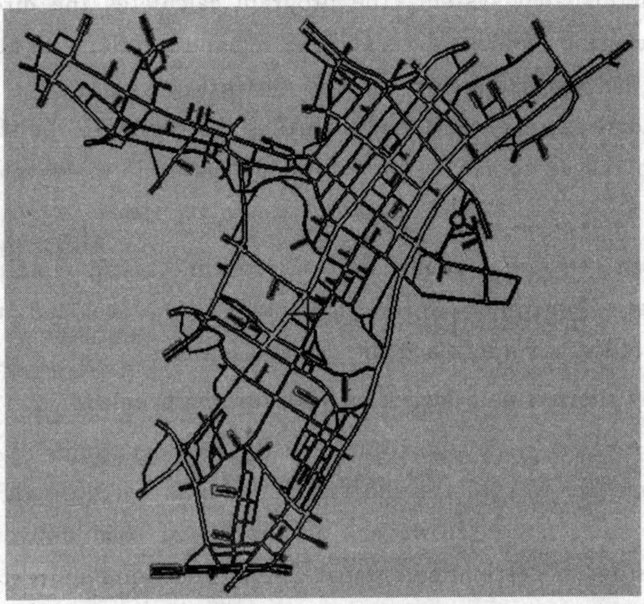

Figure 3.4 Overview of CBD Road Network

3.2.4 API Programming

An API program was developed to model the two taxi dispatch systems in the Paramics environment. The details are illustrated as follows:

1. Simulation of taxi booking and dispatch systems

The program incorporates both the existing dispatch system based on the nearest-coordinate method and the proposed dispatch system based on real-time traffic conditions. It first reads an input file containing both the demand time and the demand location, and subsequently assigns taxis based on the different dispatch mechanisms of the two systems during the simulation runs.

In the Paramics environment, the program models the roaming behavior of the empty taxis amongst the background traffic. When demand for an available taxi was generated at the designated time, on a particular link, as specified in the input file, the two systems would search for a suitable taxi based on each of their own dispatch mechanisms. Following that, each chosen taxi would be sent from its location, on the shortest time path to arrive at the demand location.

For the current dispatch system, the program calculates the direct straight-line distances between the available taxis and the demand location, by making use of the coordinates of the associated links on the network. With all the direct distances determined, the dispatch system then identifies the taxi with the shortest straight-line distance to the customer location, and delegates it to travel to the demand location.

For the proposed dispatch system based on real-time traffic conditions, a link-to-link shortest path algorithm with turning penalties was developed, to search for the shortest paths of the taxis to reach the demand location.

2. A link-to-link shortest path algorithm with turning penalties

Traditionally, shortest path algorithms usually consider nodes as the origins and destinations. In other words, the shortest path found by those algorithms is from one node to another node. However, on the actual road network, a customer location and his or her destination is most of the time along a street or a link rather than at an intersection that is represented by a node. Moreover, taxis in Singapore are prohibited from picking up or dropping off passengers at intersections, therefore the shortest path between origin and destination required here is modified to a link-to-link shortest path.

Furthermore, the characteristics of the real road networks such as the one-way links and turning restrictions imposed by traffic signal control or regulations would also prefer the shortest path algorithm based on links rather than the ones based on nodes. For example, there are usually some turning restrictions imposed at the intersections and very few shortest path algorithms in the literature have thus far incorporated the turn penalties at each node into consideration. The traditional node-based shortest path algorithms are not able to differentiate the physically connected but operationally prohibited movements. Though such a drawback can be avoided by expanding each turning movement as separate links via the so-called expanded network representation, such expansions unavoidably will incur the increase in network scale. To this end, in order to take the turning restrictions and penalties into proper accounts, a link-to-link (or link-based) shortest path algorithm is proposed and adopted. It is based on the label-setting approach, Dijkstra's algorithm (1959).

The proposed algorithm maintains and adjusts a candidate list $V:(d_1, d_2, \cdots, d_n)$ but is different from Dijkstra's algorithm in that each d_j, called the label of link j (rather than the label of node j), is either a scalar or ∞. $(a_1, a_2, \cdots, a_n)$ is the link cost of each link. In addition, this algorithm exploits another cost, incurred by the turn penalties from each link to its outgoing links: T_{ij}, i.e. the turning cost from link i to link j. In this study, T_{ij} as well as the link travel cost $(a_1, a_2, \cdots, a_n)$ are calculated and updated through simulation.

Initially, (link 1 is assumed as the origin)

$V=\{1\}$,

$d_1=0, d_i=\infty, \ \forall i\neq 1$.

The approach proceeds in iterations and terminates when the destination link is removed from list V. A typical iteration (assuming V is nonempty) is as follows:

```
Do while V is not empty
{
    Removed from the candidate list V, link i such that
     d_i = min_{j∈V} d_j
    If ( i is the destination link ) stop the iteration;
    Else
    {
       For each outgoing link j from link i, if d_j > d_i + a_j + T_ij, set
       d_j = d_i + a_j + T_ij;
       And add j to V if it does not already belong to V;
    }
}
```

The difference between the so-called node-to-node and link-to-link shortest path operations might be straightforward in the case when hypothetical or highly simplified networks are being considered. In such cases, the real street link sections, intersection delays and different travel costs of the directional links between any two nodes are usually simplified.

However, for networks in real world, the road networks usually consist of a mixture of one-way links, U-turn restrictions, traffic regulations, and the barriers along the mid-line of roads. For example, there are cases that it may take much longer time/distance for the vehicle to reach the opposite side of the street in some cases, while in some other cases, it may also be no delay at all where there is neither mid-line barrier nor U-turn restriction present at the street.

The node-based shortest path algorithm seems incompetent as compared with the link-based shortest path algorithm in order to calculate precisely the shortest path for networks with said urban settings. Note that these urban network features are usually contained in the network representation of microscopic traffic simulation. To acknowledge the need of finding shortest paths in a traffic simulation environment, the proposed link-to-link shortest path algorithm with turning penalties is adopted together accordingly.

3. Dynamic vehicle control

Although the Paramics software adopted in this research for simulation purposes, is a high performance tool with many useful functions, there is however an absence of a clear-cut function that can be used to dynamically control and simulate the routing behavior of an individual vehicle. Therefore in order to achieve dynamic vehicle control of the taxis during simulations, other characteristics and operational mechanisms of Paramics are exploited to overcome this limitation.

In Paramics software, the decision-making of a vehicle, such as that of link choices and lane changes, are actually executed by an invisible 'dummy' vehicle that is constantly located about two links ahead of the vehicle seen on the GUI during simulation runs. In this API program, in order to control the routing behavior of an individual taxi at any time during the simulation, its dummy is tracked and controlled instead. This allows the specification of the route to be taken by the taxi to reach the demand location, ensuring that the route is the one that requires the least amount of time.

4. Assumptions

In the program, it is assumed that the empty taxis roam randomly in the CBD region in wait for booking offers. It is also assumed that the empty taxi rate remains constant throughout the simulation period, that is, the number of empty available taxis within the network remains unchanged. Another assumption made is that each taxi booking received requires immediate attention from the dispatch systems to assign an appropriate taxi to the customer. The drivers of all the empty available taxis are assumed to be equally willing to accept any booking job offer.

Each taxi is also assumed to travel on its shortest time path to reach the customer after being assigned the booking job.

5. Output

The program output would account for the identity numbers of the taxis assigned the booking job, as dispatched by the two systems based on each of their own dispatch mechanisms. The locations of the assigned taxis at the instant the demand is received, and the detailed paths of taxis to reach the customer arrival will also be reported. The actual times and distances traveled by the taxis to reach the customer eventually would also be included in the output at the end of each simulation. A sample output file of the API program could be found in Appendix A.

3.2.5 Simulation Runs

With the coded networks and API program, traffic simulations are then performed to compare the performance of both dispatch systems. As each booking is independent from one another, only one booking demand will be generated and handled at an allocated time during each simulation run. Each simulation run requires an input of the demand time to simulate the time a taxi booking call is received, and a link number to indicate the location of the customer, which can be along any street within the CBD network. The time duration of each simulation run is one hour.

An allowance of 10 minutes is granted as a warm-up period, so as to ensure steady traffic flow before assigning demand and collecting data. Therefore, booking demand is generated only after 10 minutes into the simulation time. At the designated demand time, a booking request will be simulated at the specified link. As soon as the demand for a taxi is received, the search for the optimum taxi among the available taxis on the network will be launched by the two dispatch systems, based on each of their own dispatch criteria. The existing dispatch system based on the coordinate method will select the taxi with the shortest direct straight-line distance to the designated link. On the other hand, the proposed dispatch system based on real-time traffic conditions will pick the taxi with the shortest travel time to arrive at the required link. With the results generated by the API program, which includes the taxi identity numbers, direct straight-line distances from the demand location, details of paths traveled, actual travel distances and times, the dispatch solutions of both systems for each simulation run are then assessed and evaluated.

Extensive simulation runs are conducted on the CBD network to generate dispatch results of the two systems in handling booking demands in a real-life network system. The available taxi densities in the network are varied as a form of sensitivity analysis to evaluate its impact on the performance of the two systems. The empty taxi rates are varied from 5% to 15% of the total taxi fleet within the study network. Based on the data from local taxi operators in Singapore, the daily average taxi empty cruising time is 30%～35%, then it is sufficient to examine up to 15% empty taxi rate during peak hours in CBD area. For each empty taxi rate, demands are generated at 10 different locations. 10 simulation runs are conducted for each of these locations, with the demand times allocated at 5-minute intervals between simulation runs, beginning at 10 minutes into the simulation. That adds up to a total of 300 simulation runs using the CBD network. A sample screenshot of the Paramics Modeller GUI during a simulation run can be found in Figure 3.5.

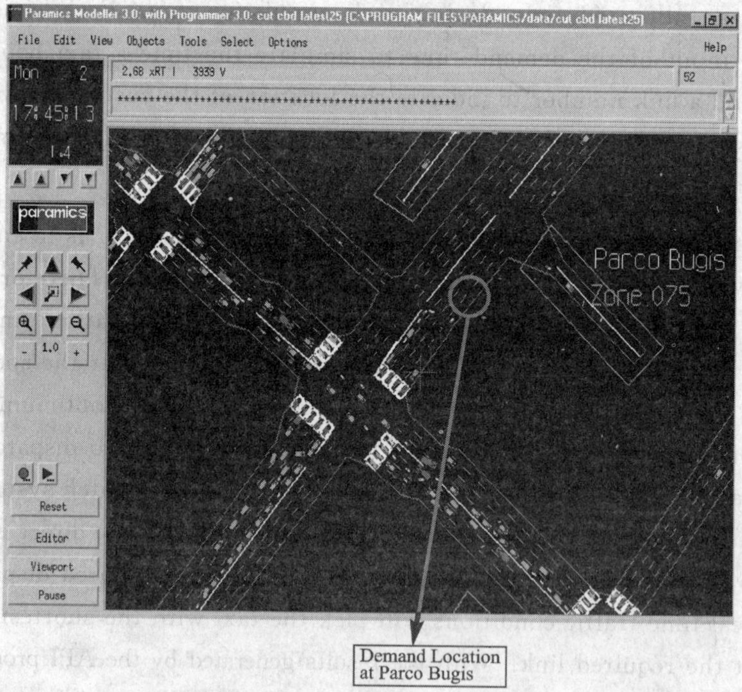

Figure 3.5 Paramics Modeler GUI during Simulation Run

With the simulation results, the performance of both systems can be assessed and evaluated. The time taken for the assigned taxi to reach the designated customer will be used as the yardstick to determine the better dispatch system out of the two. Another factor of consideration is the actual distance traveled by the taxi to reach the customer location.

3.3 RESULTS AND ANALYSIS

From the simulation runs, the necessary data required for analysis and evaluation are extracted through the API program. These results include the identity numbers of the taxis dispatched by each of the two systems, to distinguish if the two systems have identified different taxis. The direct distances of the identified taxis' locations to the customer locations are also reported, which help to verify if the current system based on the coordinate method has actually identified a taxi closer in terms of direct distance, compared to the proposed system based on real-time conditions. The actual times taken by these taxis to reach the customer location serve as the main measure of effectiveness of the two systems. (It should be noted that the simulation was running at a faster pace than real-life.) For the CBD network, the actual distances traveled by the taxis to reach the customer location will also be examined for each pair of different taxis identified.

The simulation results for a particular location at varying demand times are first presented in Section 3.3.1. This is followed by the simulation results when all the 10 locations are taken into account in Section 3.3.2. The simulation results for varying empty taxi rates are then discussed in Section 3.3.3.

3.3.1 Variation of Demand Times

As aforementioned, the background traffic is set according to the OD data provided by the LTA. The total number of taxis is assumed to be approximately 2,000 roaming at anytime within CBD area, based on information obtained from both LTA and the taxi companies. The empty taxi rate is initially set at 5% of the total taxi population, which means that at any one time during the simulation period, there are 100 empty taxis available for serving customer-booking demands in the CBD area. The demand location is first fixed at Parco Bugis, which is a popular shopping area in the CBD region. The demand times are varied in 5-minute intervals for the 10 simulation runs. The simulation results obtained are tabulated in Table 3.1.

Table 3.1 Simulation Results with Demand Location at Parco Bugis

Run No.	Taxi Identified	Direct Distance/m		Actual Travel Time/s	
		Current System	Proposed System	Current System	Proposed System
1	Different	34	406	144	11
2	Different	124	587	139	34
3	Same	34	34	149	149
4	Different	104	352	303	66
5	Different	181	635	157	57
6	Different	34	352	290	67
7	Different	211	520	132	86
8	Different	0	539	242	34
9	Different	39	406	292	13
10	Different	94	533	152	68
Average		86	436	200	58

From Table 3.1, it may be observed that there are 9 out of 10 instances where a different taxi is identified by the proposed dispatch system based on real-time traffic conditions. There is only one occasion where an identical taxi is identified. For run no. 8, it can be seen that the direct distance of the taxi identified by the current system is '0' meter and yet it takes a longer time than the other taxi identified by the proposed system, to reach the customer location. This could be due to two possibilities; one is that the taxi is on the opposite side of the road traveling in the opposite direction. The other possibility is that the taxi has just past the customer location at the instant the booking is received. Hence, to get back to the customer, the taxi has to make a detour, taking a much longer time as a result. And for each of the other 9 instances, where different taxis are identified by the two systems, the travel times for the proposed system are always shorter than that for the current system.

The differences in the travel times of the taxis dispatched by the two systems are illustrated in Figure 3. 6. It can be observed that the times taken by the taxis dispatched by the proposed system is always less than or equal to the times taken by the taxis dispatched by the current system. The only occurrence when the two times are equal represents run number 3 where the taxi identified by the proposed system coincides with the taxi identified by the current system.

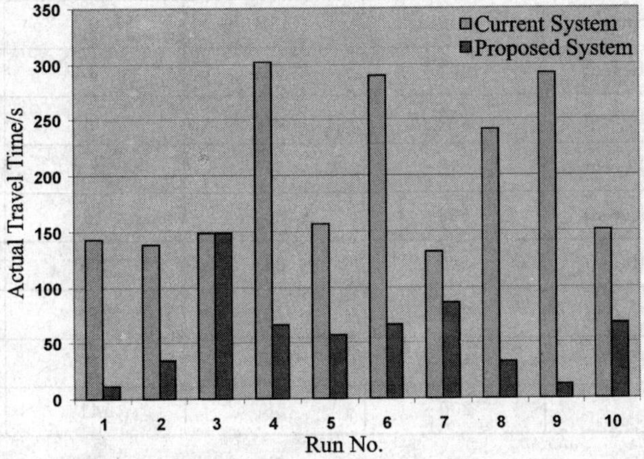

Figure 3. 6 Comparison of Actual Travel Times with Demand Location at Parco

It can be seen from Table 3. 2 that with this proposed system, the times taken for the assigned taxis to arrive at the demand locations are significantly reduced. The improvements in travel times range from 35. 0% to a high of 95. 7% of the timings taken by taxis dispatched via the current system, with the average of a 70. 8% reduction. Besides the time factor, a comparison is also made based on the actual distances traveled by the assigned taxis to reach the customer location. The relevant figures are tabulated in Table 3. 3. It can be observed that whenever the proposed system brings about an improvement in times required for the assigned taxis to reach the customer location, it also reduces the actual distances traveled significantly. The average improvement in distance is about 54. 7% of the average actual distances for the taxis dispatched by the current system. Therefore, the proposed system is definitely more efficient than the current system in dispatching taxis to serve bookings at the location of Parco Bugis.

Table 3.2 Actual Travel Times with Demand Location at Parco Bugis

Run No.	Taxi Identified	Travel Time/s		Improvement in Time	
		Current System	Proposed System	sec	%
1	Different	144	11	133	92.3
2	Different	139	34	105	75.5
3	Same	149	149	0	0.0
4	Different	303	66	237	78.2
5	Different	157	57	100	63.6
6	Different	290	67	223	77.0
7	Different	132	86	46	35.0
8	Different	242	34	208	86.1
9	Different	292	13	279	95.7
10	Different	152	68	84	55.1
Average		200	58	141	70.8

Table 3.3 Actual Travel Distances with Demand Location at Parco Bugis

Run No.	Taxi Identified	Travel Distance/m		Improvementin Distance	
		Current System	Proposed System	m	%
1	Different	1263	1223	39	3.1
2	Different	1263	164	1099	87.0
3	Same	—	—	0	0.0
4	Different	1263	164	1099	87.0
5	Different	1263	1216	46	3.7
6	Different	1174	164	1010	86.0
7	Different	1263	164	1099	87.0
8	Different	1263	110	1153	91.3
9	Different	1228	356	872	71.0
10	Different	1461	929	531	36.4
Average		1271	499	695	54.7

3.3.2 Variation of Demand Locations

With the empty taxi rate fixed at 5%, nine other locations are investigated. These demand locations include other popular areas in the CBD, such as Raffles Place, Shenton Way, Chinatown and Orchard Road, where there are frequent requests for taxi booking services. The locations of these 10 areas on the network can be found in Figure 3.7. Again, for each location, 10 simulation runs are conducted with the demand generated at 10 different time intervals. Results favoring the proposed system, similar to those for the location of Parco Bugis, are obtained at each of these other 9 locations. Detailed simulation results for each of the locations are found in Appendix B. A summary of the improvements in time at the 10 locations is tabulated in Table 3.4. The differences in the amounts of time required for the taxis dispatched by the two systems are also illustrated in Figure 3.8.

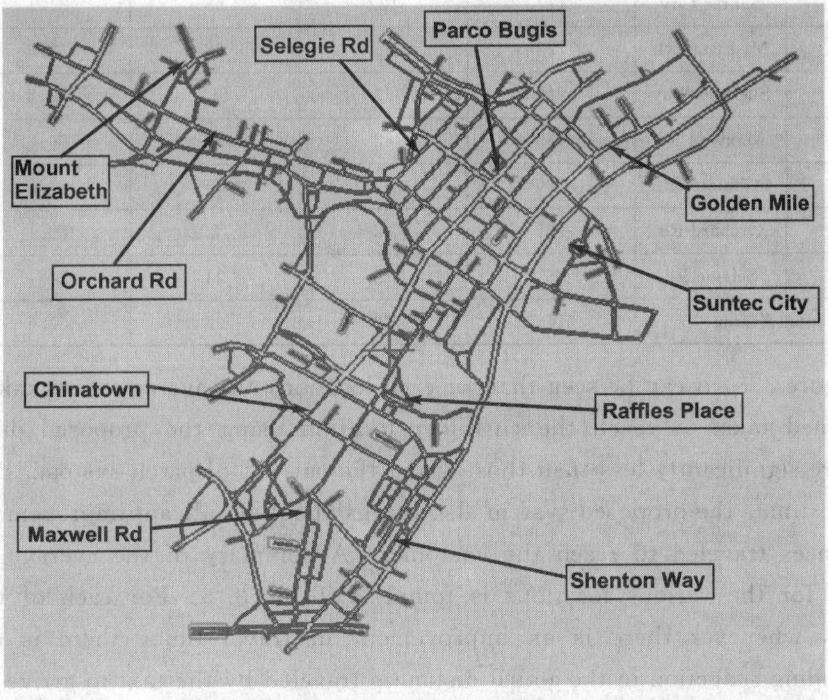

Figure 3.7 Demand Locations within CBD Network

It can be observed from Table 3.4 that the performance level of the proposed system is higher than the current system, with average time improvements for all 10 locations. The average improvements in time range from 24.7% for Selegie Road to 80.1% for Orchard Road. With the proposed system based on real-time traffic conditions, the total average improvement in time for all the 10 locations is 53.6% of the total average time taken by the taxis dispatched by the current system based on the current system based on the coordinate method.

Table 3.4 Time Improvements of Various Demand Locations

Location No.	Demand Location	Average Travel Time/s		Average Improvement in Time	
		Current System	Proposed System	sec	%
1	Parco Bugis	200	58	142	71.0
2	Golden Mile	228	162	66	28.9
3	Raffles Place	196	87	109	55.6
4	Suntec City	177	122	55	31.1
5	Mt Elizabeth	123	55	68	55.3
6	Shenton Way	216	63	153	70.8
7	Maxwell Rd	155	62	93	60.0
8	Chinatown	126	62	65	51.6
9	Orchard Rd	161	32	129	80.1
10	Selegie Rd	97	73	24	24.7
Total Average		168	78	90	53.6

From Figure 3.8, it can be seen that for each location, the average times taken for the assigned taxis to reach the customer location using the proposed dispatch system are significantly less than those using the current dispatch system. Besides savings in time, the proposed system also brings about significant improvements in the distances traveled to reach the customer. A summary of the average travel distances for the various locations is found in Table 3.5. For each of the 10 locations, whenever there is an improvement in travel time, there is also a corresponding reduction in the actual distances traveled by the taxi to arrive at the customer locations. The total average improvement in distance for the 10 locations is about 53.2% of the total average travel distances for the taxis dispatched by the current system.

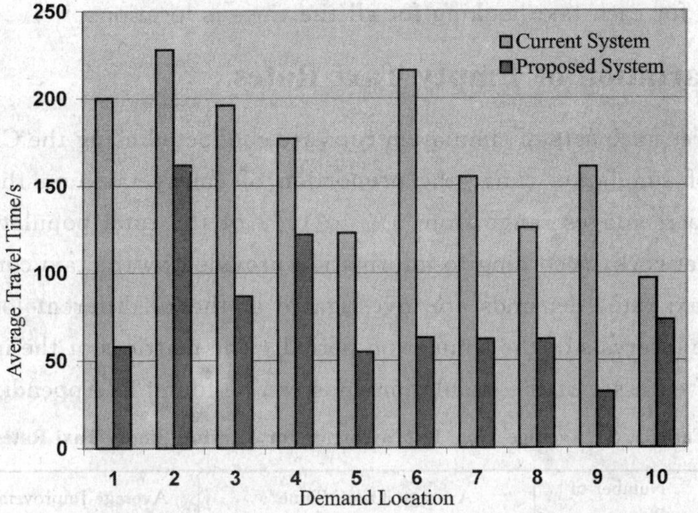

Figure 3. 8 Comparisons of Average Travel Times at Various Locations

Table 3. 5 Simulation Results of Various Demand Locations

Location No.	Demand Location	Average Travel Distance/m		Average Improvement in Distance	
		Current System	Proposed System	m	%
1	Parco Bugis	1271	499	772	60. 7
2	Golden Mile	2656	1590	1066	40. 1
3	Raffles Place	1679	625	1056	62. 8
4	Suntec City	1860	1042	818	44. 0
5	Mt Elizabeth	1059	496	563	53. 2
6	Shenton Way	2222	1007	1215	54. 7
7	Maxwell Rd	1745	623	1122	64. 3
8	Chinatown	1411	805	606	43. 0
9	Orchard Rd	1487	445	1042	70. 1
10	Selegie Rd	1123	593	530	47. 2
Total Average		1651	772	879	53. 2

Therefore, other than significant improvements in time, the proposed dispatch system also brings considerable reductions in the travel distance. Hence, the proposed system is clearly more efficient in the dispatch of taxis, bringing a better match of taxi for each taxi booking for all the various locations.

3.3.3 Variation of Empty Taxi Rates

A total of three such sets of simulation runs are conducted using the CBD network. In each set of simulation runs, the proportion of empty taxis on the network is varied. The percentages range from 5% to 15% of the total population of 2,000 taxis in the network, according to information provided by the taxi companies. For each empty-taxi rate, demands are investigated at the 10 different locations at 10 different time intervals of the simulation period. The matrices of the improvements in time for of each set of the simulation runs can be found in Appendix C.

Table 3.6 Average Time Improvements for Varying Empty Taxi Rates

Empty Taxi Rate/(%)	Number of Available Empty Taxis	Average Travel Time/s		Average Improvement in Time	
		Current System	Proposed System	sec	%
5	100	168	78	90	53.6
10	200	154	62	92	59.8
15	300	146	59	87	59.6
Total Average		156	66	90	57.7

The simulation results for these three sets of results are summarized in Table 3.6. It can be observed that for varying empty taxi rates, there are always average time improvements with the usage of the proposed dispatch system based on real-time traffic conditions. Plotting the average travel times against the empty taxi rates gives the graph in Figure 3.9.

From Figure 3.9, it can be seen that for each empty taxi rate, the average travel time for the taxis dispatched by the proposed system are less than that of the taxis dispatched by the current system. Therefore, the proposed system proves to be more efficient than the current system for varying empty taxi rates. It can also be observed as the empty taxi rate increases from 5% to 15%, the average travel times for both systems decreases. This is because as there are more and more empty taxis to serve the booking customers, both the current and proposed systems are able to identify taxis with shorter direct distances and shorter time paths to the customer locations. This indicates a better choice of the optimal taxi as the empty taxi rate

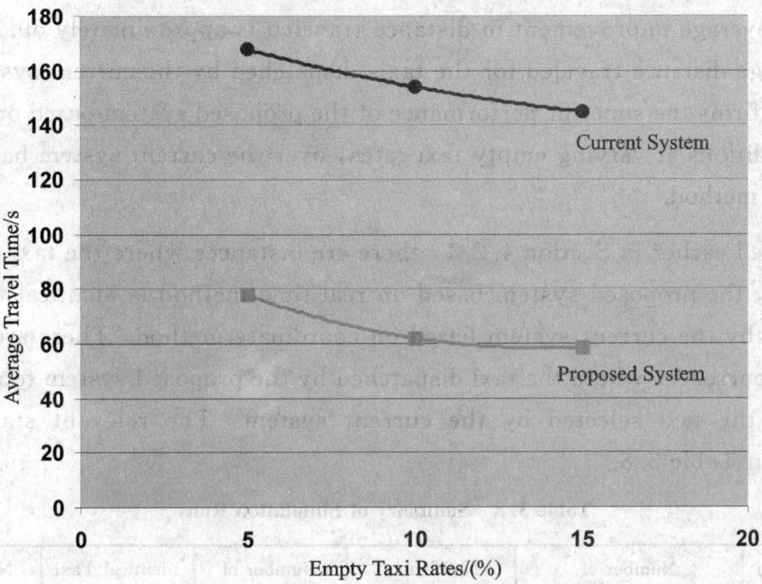

Figure 3. 9 Variation of Average Travel Times with Empty Taxi Rates

increases. It may also be noticed that for all the variation in rates, the average travel times of the taxis dispatched by the proposed system based on real-time method is considerably less than that of the taxis dispatched by the current system based on the coordinate method.

It can be seen from Table 3. 6 that the average improvement in time for all three empty taxi rates is 90 seconds, which is about 57. 7% of the average travel time of the taxis dispatched by the coordinate system. Together with average time improvements, the proposed system also brings about considerable savings in distances, as can be seen in Table 3. 7.

Table 3. 7 Average Distance Improvements for Varying Empty Taxi Rates

Empty Taxi Rate/(%)	Number of Available Empty Taxis	Average Travel Distance/m		Average Improvement in Distance	
		Current System	Proposed System	m	%
5	100	1651	772	879	53. 2
10	200	1644	647	997	60. 6
15	300	1572	572	1000	63. 6
Total Average		1408	681	958	59. 2

The total average improvement in distance traveled is approximately 59.2% of the total average distance traveled for the taxis dispatched by the current system. This again, reaffirms the superior performance of the proposed system based on real-time traffic conditions at varying empty taxi rates, over the current system based on the coordinate method.

As discussed earlier in Section 4.2.1, there are instances where the taxi chosen for dispatch by the proposed system based on real-time method is identical to the taxi dispatched by the current system based on coordinate method. There are also rare adverse occurrences where the taxi dispatched by the proposed system took a longer time than the taxi selected by the current system. The relevant statistics are tabulated in Table 3.8.

Table 3.8 Summary of Simulation Runs

Empty Taxi Rate/(%)	Number of Available Empty Taxis	Number of Simulation Runs	Number of Positive Cases	Identical Taxi Occurrences	Number of Adverse Cases
5	100	100	71	27	2
10	200	100	69	29	2
15	300	100	70	26	4
Total	300	210	82	8	

From Table 3.8, it can be seen that among the 300 simulation runs conducted, there are 210 cases where the proposed system identified a faster taxi, 82 cases where it identified the same taxi, and 8 cases where it identified a slower taxi. That means the proposed system is more efficient 70% of the time, as efficient 27% of the time, and less efficient only 3% of the time, than the current system. For the 3% of adverse cases, the reason for a slower taxi is due to disparity between the instantaneous and the actual travel times experienced (as known as ideal travel time, based on predictive traffic conditions). This is most probably caused by a change in the traffic conditions while the taxi is on its way to the customer location, resulting in it to take a longer travel time. However, these occurrences are rare, occurring only 8 times out of the 300 simulation runs.

Thus it may be concluded that the performance level of proposed system based on the real-time traffic conditions is indeed superior to the current system based on the coordinate method. With the proposed system, not only is the amount of customer waiting time is effectively decreased under all the general circumstances considered, the distance that the assigned taxi has to travel to reach the customer is also significantly reduced.

3.4 SUMMARY

This study investigates the effectiveness of the existing dispatch system based on nearest-coordinate method in comparison to the proposed dispatch system based on instantaneous traffic conditions. Through the Paramics simulation model based on the CBD network, the potential benefits of the proposed dispatching method are demonstrated and evaluated.

From the analysis of the simulation results, it is clear that the proposed system yields significant time savings in meeting customer bookings. This effectively reduces the amount of customer waiting time, as each customer would be served within the shortest period of time possible by the most suitable taxi, thus increasing customer satisfaction. Besides benefiting the customers, taxi drivers also stand to gain from this proposed system. With a decrease in traveling times to reach the booking customers, the empty cruise times of the taxis are also shortened as a result. Moreover, the distances that the assigned taxis have to travel to reach the customer are also significantly reduced. This will help the taxi drivers cut down any unnecessary diesel consumption.

On the whole, this proposed system will enable taxi companies to reduce the passenger pick up time, hence improving the accuracy and efficiency of their dispatch systems, so as to deliver a higher level of service to the customers. With a reduction in the waiting times, more customers would be willing to hire taxis through bookings, rather than to use other means of hiring. This will allow the taxi operators to better manage and optimize their taxi fleet, as a better match of taxi demand and supply could then be met.

CHAPTER 4
TRIP-CHAINING FOR TAXI ADVANCE BOOKINGS

This part is the extension of Chapter 3.

4.1 INTRODUCTION

As mentioned earlier, there are in general two types of booking services provided by taxi companies in Singapore, current and advance. Chapter 3 presented in detail a new dispatch system for current booking demands. While in this chapter, the focal point was on the advance bookings, where this real-life problem was specially defined as STAR, the short form of Singapore Taxi Advance Reservation. A novel trip-chaining strategy for taxi advance booking based on a customized algorithm of Pickup and Delivery Problem with Time Window (PDPTW) was proposed. Based on the experimental results, the proposed system would reduce the taxi fleet size by up to 87.5%, in serving the same level of advance booking demands. The trip-chaining strategy proposed has the potential to change the concept of the taxi booking service currently operating in Singapore. Not only will this result in more reasonable price structures for taxi services, but also bring benefits to customers, drivers and taxi companies.

The chapter is organized as follows. Following this introduction, a description of the existing dispatch system and its deficiencies is presented. The proposed dispatch system for the taxi advance booking service is presented in the next section. This is followed by sections which illustrate the methodology of the new system, which includes the paired Pickup and Delivery with Time Window (PDPTW) models; a review of accessible related literature; the problem of Singapore Taxi Advance Reservation (STAR) with its special requirements, which is based on the actual booking services in Singapore; a customized two-phase method; the study network as well as Application Program Interface (API) programming for traffic simulations. The results of simulation experiments are subsequently presented, followed by a discussion on the performance of the proposed system. Finally, the benefits of the proposed system for customers, drivers and taxi companies are highlighted in the summary of this chapter.

4.2 THE EXISTING DISPATCH SYSTEM AND ITS DEFICIENCIES

Once an advance booking demand is made, the dispatching center broadcasts this booking information immediately to the island-wide taxi network in Singapore, to both occupied and empty taxis, since the advance bookings are services which should be fulfilled at least half an hour later. The job is assigned to the first taxi driver who bids for it.

Obviously, under this dispatch system, advance bookings are handled on a case-by-case basis; and booking demands are treated/assigned independently. For instance, up to 100 different taxis might be assigned to fulfill an equal number of bookings. Hence, the taxi supply resource, in terms of occupancy time, may not be significantly utilized.

At the same time, one advance-booking request usually affects a taxi's street pickup service. In fact, taxi drivers often face a dilemma when the time for an advance-booking job is approximately 30 minutes later. In other words, if a driver tries to pick up roadside passengers, then the booking job may not be fulfilled on time. Conversely, if the driver gives up all the street pickup business, then it is apparently a waste of time and vehicle resource. This situation has been used by taxi companies to justify why the surcharge for advance bookings is higher than that of current bookings in Singapore (see Table 2.1).

As a result, customers have to bear with an unreasonable price structure, which appears irrational with daily experiences elsewhere. For instance, early bookings for hotel rooms or air travels always entail discounts. From the consumers' point of view, it clearly makes no sense to have a higher surcharge for advance booking than current booking for taxis.

However, under the current taxi booking surcharge structure, a customer will pay more if he/she books a taxi earlier for a planned trip. Hence, to some extent, customers are encouraged to use taxi services at the last minute, either through street hailing or through current-bookings, to avoid paying higher advance-booking fees. However, it is known that this will cause the customer to be involved in risks such as taking a long time to find an empty taxi through street hailing. Finally, customers faced with time constraints have to give up waiting and switch to and pay for current-booking services. Nevertheless, the fact is that even the current-booking system cannot offer a hundred percent guarantee of obtaining a taxi service quickly during certain time periods.

Therefore, the above-mentioned direct or indirect problems are essentially due to available customers' advance-booking information that has not been well exploited by the existing dispatch system. Hence, new taxi dispatch systems that can deal with such problems become an urgent priority.

4.3 THE PROPOSED DISPATCH SYSTEM FOR ADVANCE BOOKINGS

Based on the data provided by local taxi operators in Singapore, nearly 40 advance-booking demands are made every five minutes during the peak hours (from 7:00 to 9:30 in the morning and from 16:30 to 19:00 in the evening). To take full advantage of the aforementioned taxi supply resource, chained trips may be planned and offered to taxi drivers as a package. This means that several bookings with demand times points that are spread out within a reasonable period of time can be chained, provided that each pick-up point coincides with or is within close proximity to the previous drop-off location. The shortest time paths as generated by the proposed dispatch system based on real-life traffic conditions for each job, could perhaps be linked up to form properly planned routes to be offered as a multiple-booking package to taxi drivers. This will help the drivers to minimize their empty cruising times, as the time will be spent fulfilling these advanced demands instead of cruising around in search of street-hailing customers.

were incompatible with vehicle capacity, precedence and time window constraints.

The multiple-vehicle pickup and delivery problem with time windows has received little attention. The only optimal algorithm developed by Dumas *et al*. (1991) employed a column generation scheme with a shortest-path sub-problem with capacity, time window, precedence and coupling constraints. The algorithm can solve 1-PDPTW problems of up to 55 paired requests and multiple-vehicle PDPTW with a small number of paired requests per vehicle.

Recently, William and Barnes (2000) proposed a reactive tabu search approach to minimize travel cost by using a penalty objective function in terms of travel time, penalty for violation of overload and time window constraints. The approach was tested on instances with sizes of 25, 50 and 100 customers. These test cases were constructed from Solomon's C1 VRPTW benchmark instances (Solomon 1987), which were solved optimally.

More recently, researchers such as Lau and Liang (2002), Li and Lim (2001) have generated many test cases for PDPTW from Solomon's benchmark instances initially designed for VRPTW and proposed their different versions of Tabu-Search embedded Meta-Heuristics to solve PDPTW, each with good results.

4.4.3 The Problem and Its Special Requirements

This section analyzes the problem as defined by the authors of this paper as the Singapore Taxi Advance Reservations (STAR) problem. Based on the characteristics of the taxi booking service currently operating in Singapore, the differences between the STAR as addressed here, and the normal PDPTW in literature, are as follows:

i. Multiple vehicles are made available all over the street network instead of starting from a central depot.

ii. Pickup and delivery jobs are paired and directly connected without any interruption from other pickup or delivery jobs.

iii. Hard and extremely narrow-time window, i.e. a desired pickup time point with few deviations, has to be satisfied instead of a time window with earliest and latest allowable pickup time. Usually, a desired pickup time point is requested by a customer. A customer will complain if he is forced to wait for more than

2-3 minutes beyond the pickup time point for the taxi that has been booked by him in advance.

ⅳ. Vehicle capacity constraint is automatically respected by the customers. In real life a customer will consider this constraint when specifying the number of taxis to be booked.

ⅴ. Short response time for the solution.

To adopt a PDPTW model for the solution of the STAR problem, the computational cost is a critical factor, since customers cannot wait for more than a few minutes to receive a confirmation on his/her booking request, and the algorithm is supposed to be implemented in a dynamic environment intended for on-line scheduling.

At the time of the planning, the following information was available:

ⅰ. A number of requests for taxi service are identified in advance at each planning horizon.

ⅱ. For each customer the following information is known:

a. The pickup location requested by the customer

b. The delivery destination of the trip

c. The desired pickup time.

ⅲ. The driving distances between the above-mentioned locations are well understood. Furthermore, the driving times between each Origin-Destination pair are based on data calculated through microscopic traffic simulations.

ⅳ. The average service time is based on daily statistics data, i. e. the time consumed when customers get on board, pay for the bill and alight from the vehicle.

There are a wide variety of objective functions for PDPTW. In the problem of STAR, the following were considered:

ⅰ. Minimizing the number of vehicles, which is the most dominant part of the costs for taxi operators.

ⅱ. Minimizing travel time/distance, i. e. , the sum of the driving times or the length of all the routes in the plan, which is usually the main input of fuel consumption.

To model the duo-objective of minimizing (a) the total number of vehicles and (b) total travel time/distance as a linear function, a coefficient for each objective was multiplied and then added together. Since the number of vehicles is more important than the total travel time of a plan, the cost of each vehicle (route) is penalized with a coefficient C, which is set to be greater than the maximum possible total travel time. Hence, the objective function of the problem is:

$$\text{Minimize } C \times m + f(R)$$

Where, m is the total number of taxi used, and R is a pickup and delivery route plan, $f(R)$ is defined as the total travel cost (driving time or distance). The first term in the above objective function may be considered as the fixed cost and the second term as the variable cost.

4.4.3 The Customized Two-Phase Method

It has been shown that a successful approach for solving PDPTW is to construct an initial set of feasible routes that serve all the customers (construction phase) and subsequently improve the existing solution (improvement phase) (Gendreau *et al*. 1994, Glover and Laguna 1997, Golden and Assad 1988). This is known as the two-phase method.

However, the characteristics and requirements of STAR preclude straightforward implementation of most algorithms that have been developed for the normal VRPTW or PDPTW. In this section, a two-phase method for solving STAR is proposed. This two-phase method comprises the *Insertion algorithm and the Tabu Search*.

1. The Construction Phase

Nearest-neighbor heuristics, sweep heuristics, and least-cost insertion algorithm are well-known heuristics for constructing a feasible solution for the class of vehicle routing problems.

Nearest-neighbor heuristics adds on the closest customer for extending the trip, i.e., at each step, the trip is built by adding the customer closest to the point last visited by the vehicle until all customers have been visited. In this heuristics, a new vehicle is introduced when the current vehicle in use cannot accommodate more customers.

Sweep heuristics is another well-known construction heuristic method for vehicle routing and scheduling. It builds routes by using a sweep technique around a certain location. The sweep heuristic for VRP is shown below:

ⅰ. Let O be a site (usually the depot in literature), which serves as a central point, and let A (different from O) be another location, which serves as a reference.

ⅱ. Sort jobs by increasing angle $\angle AOJ$ where J is the job location. Place the result in a list L.

ⅲ. The jobs in L will be allocated to the vehicles in the above order as long as constraints are respected.

For the least-cost greedy insertion method, this iterative algorithm has to compute the cost (the resultant increment in travel time/distance) of inserting every new customer into every feasible insertion position in every route that has been built so far, and then an insertion is performed with the minimum incremental cost. Obviously, the computation cost is much higher than nearest-neighbor heuristics or sweep heuristics when the problem size is close to a real life situation.

In contrast to the common PDPTW problems, the time windows of taxi booking demands are extremely narrow; i. e., customers who make an advance booking usually specify the time 'point' instead of the time 'window'. Hence, the construction heuristics in the literature may not be efficient for solving such problems as taxi dispatching. In the first phase, the earliest time window insertion algorithm was proposed for the 'ad hoc' problem of taxi dispatching, which was then compared with nearest-neighbor heuristics and sweep heuristics in the section on experimental results.

The proposed earliest time window insertion algorithm is an iterative approach with the following steps:

ⅰ. Let all vehicles have empty routes (with no booking assignments initially).

ⅱ. Let L be the list of unassigned requests.

ⅲ. Take a job pair v in which the requested passenger pickup time is the earliest from the current list of L.

ⅳ. Insert v in a route at a feasible position.

ⅴ. Remove v from L.

ⅵ. If L is not empty, go to 3.

The initial feasible solution is then improved in the improvement phase.

2. The Improvement Phase

A tabu search was performed to improve the solution given by the insertion algorithm described above. In this study, the steepest decent search was applied. A move in this approach corresponds to one of the traditional vehicle-routing move operations. In this study, the focus was on two types of move operations, namely *exchange and relocate*.

An exchange operation swaps two different existing routes, whereas in a relocate operation, a customer is removed from the original route and reinserted into an existing route (it could be the same route but at a different position). A move is considered feasible if the corresponding operation does not violate any requirement (for instance, time constraints) in PDPTW. Hence the neighborhood of the current solution is defined by all the feasible moves. In each iteration of the steepest decent approach, the feasible move that gives the best improvement (or least deterioration) of the cost is selected.

To avoid the search from revisiting the same solution in the near future, the tabu search mechanism was introduced. A *tabu list* that recorded the n previous moves performed was maintained in memory. A move was considered tabu if it was in the tabu list. Moreover, a move was 'aspired' if the resultant cost was lower than the cost of the best solution encountered.

If the best move selected by the steepest decent approach was tabu and not aspired, then the next best move in the neighborhood of the current solution would be considered; otherwise, the selected move was made. The improvement process in this phase continued until a pre-set maximum number of iterations *maxIter* was reached or a pre-set maximum computation time *maxTime* had been performed. The key steps of the improvement phase are given as follows:

ⅰ. Let the current solution x be the feasible solution generated in the construction phase, and set the solution of 'best so far' $z^* = \infty$.

ⅱ. Choose the best move *bestMove* from the neighborhood of the current solution.

ⅲ. If *bestMove* is tabu and not aspired, let *bestMove* be the next best move in the neighborhood and go to Step 3, otherwise accept *bestMove* and update the solution x and cost $z(x)$.

ⅳ. If $z(x)<z^*$, then $x^*=x$ and $z^*=z(x)$.

ⅴ. Repeat step 2 to 4 until the number of iterations equals *maxIter* or until *maxTime* computation time has been performed.

ⅵ. Output x^* and z^*.

4.4.5 The Study Network

Instead of using centroids and constant travel costs between pick-up and drop-off locations as was reported in literature, a customized microscopic simulation model, PARAMICS, was again adopted to model real-street-network traffic conditions.

A portion of the Central Business District (CBD) area in Singapore (Figure 3.4) was yet again selected as the study network in this study; the reason has been addressed in the previous chapter.

4.4.6 Application Program Interface (API) Program for Traffic Simulation

An API program was developed to collect the travel time of each link along the CBD network through traffic simulations. A link-to-link shortest path algorithm was embedded into the API program to search for the shortest time paths for each origin-destination pair.

Forty pairs of pick-up and drop-off locations were selected at major trip generators, e.g., shopping malls, hospitals and convention centers. Twelve sets of booking demands were randomly generated with pickup time points between the afternoon peak hours and midnight of the same day, and pickup and drop off locations distributed among the forty pairs of trip generators (See Table 4.1 and Table 4.2).

Table 4.1 One Set of Randomly Generated Demand

Booking Request	Pickup Location	Destination Location	Pickup Time
1	The Paragon Tower	Parco Bugis Junction	9:30 PM
2	Cairnhill Place	Bank of China	9:55 PM

Table 4.1 (Continued)

Booking Request	Pickup Location	Destination Location	Pickup Time
3	Sunshine Plaza	People's Park Complex	11:40 PM
4	Sin Tai Hin Building	Centennial Tower	8:35 PM
5	Parco Bugis Junction	Maxwell Road Food Center	8:25 PM
6	Bugis Village	UIC Building	8:25 PM
7	Golden Mile Complex	Air View Building	7:35 PM
8	Keypoint Building	People's Park Complex	10:30 PM
9	Ngee Ann City	OUB Center	8:25 PM
10	Singapore Power Building	Centennial Tower	6:10 PM
11	Suntec City Tower	Sunshine Plaza	8:50 PM
12	Centennial Tower	Air View Building	7:45 PM
13	People's Park Complex	Ngee Ann City	8:05 PM
14	Ministry of Manpower	Golden Mile Complex	10:00 PM
15	OUB Center	The Paragon Tower	9:45 PM
16	Bank of China	Golden Mile Complex	8:10 PM
17	Maxwell Road Food Center	CPF Building	8:05 PM
18	Air View Building	Sin Tai Hin Building	9:30 PM
19	CPF Building	Ngee Ann City	6:10 PM
20	UIC Building	Bugis Village	8:50 PM
21	Cairnhill Place	People's Park Complex	6:45 PM
22	The Paragon Tower	Centennial Tower	8:50 PM
23	Sunshine Plaza	Air View Building	9:10 PM
24	Sin Tai Hin Building	CPF Building	8:00 PM
25	Parco Bugis Junction	Cairnhill Place	9:40 PM
26	Bugis Village	People's Park Complex	8:00 PM
27	Golden Mile Complex	Parco Bugis Junction	6:30 PM
28	Keypoint Building	Bank of China	10:50 PM
29	Singapore Power Building	Sunshine Plaza	9:05 PM

Table 4.1 (Continued)

Booking Request	Pickup Location	Destination Location	Pickup Time
30	Ngee Ann City	Air View Building	10:40 PM
31	Centennial Tower	Ngee Ann City	8:35 PM
32	Suntec City Tower	Golden Mile Complex	8:45 PM
33	Ministry of Manpower	OUB Center	9:55 PM
34	People's Park Complex	Centennial Tower	6:55 PM
35	Bank of China	CPF Building	6:55 PM
36	OUB Center	Sin Tai Hin Building	8:20 PM
37	Air View Building	Ngee Ann City	8:10 PM
38	Maxwell Road Food Center	Bugis Village	6:55 PM
39	UIC Building	The Paragon Tower	7:50 PM
40	CPF Building	Golden Mile Complex	8:40 PM
Average Deviation of Pickup Time: $\sum_{i=1}^{n} \mid T_i - \overline{T} \mid /n$			59.5 (min)

Table 4.2 Randomly Generated Demand Sets with Different Pickup Time Deviations

Booking Demand Set	1	2	3	4	5	6	7	8	9	10	11	12
Average Deviation of Pickup Time/min	15.1	23.6	30.6	46.4	59.5	64.1	74.5	88.4	94.7	107.6	111.5	123.9

Each demand set represents the advance-booking requests that the dispatch system receives in five minutes. For each demand set, the time deviation is defined as $\sum_{i=1}^{n} \mid T_i - \overline{T} \mid /n$, where T_i is the desired pickup time point and $\overline{T}$ stands for the average pickup time. Twelve demand sets were then randomly generated (see Appendix D), with the average deviation of requested pickup time for each booking set varying from 15 minutes to two hours. To study the performance of these heuristics, the pickup time deviation could not be too slight during the experiment. This is because an extremely small deviation means all the booking demands are requested for almost the same (or nearly the same) pickup time, and thus there is very limited opportunity to chain these trips.

4.5 EXPERIMENTAL RESULTS

Numerical comparisons between the proposed insertion algorithm and other construction heuristics, i. e. nearest neighbor insertion heuristics and sweep insertion heuristics were first conducted (See Table 4. 3). All the computation works were carried out in a personal computer with a Pentium IV 1. 8 GHz CPU and 512 MB of RAM. The computation times of these construction heuristics were always less than one second to get the initial solution with a problem size of forty booking jobs in this study. Then each of these initial solutions was improved by using the same Tabu search procedure within the same computation time of five seconds (pre-set maximum computation time for the improvement phase). The results are shown in Table 4. 4.

From Table 4. 3, it can be observed that the initial solution from the proposed earliest time insert heuristics was significantly better than the other two heuristics (nearest neighbor insertion and sweep insertion) in terms of the number of taxis required. However, a smaller number of routes would increase the total travel costs. This is because the calculation of travel cost of each route involved in this study began with the origin of the first booking demand and ended with the destination of the last booking demand, and included all the travel costs between these connected demands. Therefore, with fewer routes made, a greater demand would be induced within each route, thus increasing travel costs between connected demands.

Table 4. 3 Initial Solutions

Table 4. 3. 1 Initial Solutions by Heuristics Based on Nearest Neighbor Insertion

No.	1	2	3	4	5	6	7	8	9	10	11	12	Average
Pickup Time Deviation/min	15. 1	23. 6	30. 6	46. 4	59. 5	64. 1	74. 5	88. 4	94. 7	107. 6	111. 5	123. 9	
Taxi Used	16	12	11	9	9	12	9	10	9	10	9	10	10. 50
Total Travel Cost/min	229. 2	245. 6	240. 2	239. 1	249. 3	235. 4	233. 2	254. 6	235. 8	231. 0	248. 2	241. 8	240. 3

Table 4.3.2 Initial Solutions by Heuristics Based on Sweep Insertion

No.	1	2	3	4	5	6	7	8	9	10	11	12	Average
Pickup Time Deviation/min	15.1	23.6	30.6	46.4	59.5	64.1	74.5	88.4	94.7	107.6	111.5	123.9	
Taxi Used	15	12	11	10	10	14	9	11	8	11	10	11	11.00
Total Travel Cost/min	232.5	242.3	248.9	245.7	246.0	231.7	238.6	244.4	234.2	235.7	261.6	242.9	242.0

Table 4.3.3 Initial Solutions by Heuristics Based on Earliest Time Insertion

No.	1	2	3	4	5	6	7	8	9	10	11	12	Average
Pickup Time Deviation/min	15.1	23.6	30.6	46.4	59.5	64.1	74.5	88.4	94.7	107.6	111.5	123.9	
Taxi Used	10	7	7	5	4	5	4	5	3	4	4	4	5.17
Total Travel Cost/min	283.1	286.2	286.2	304.7	297.0	292.2	300.2	307.0	300.7	306.1	308.1	310.2	298.5

The sweep heuristics seems to be inferior to both the nearest neighbor insertion method and the earliest time insertion method. However, the advantage of sweep heuristics is that near and far jobs are mixed in the same route. This makes the solution more balanced, i.e. there are no extremely good routes or extremely bad ones between drivers.

In an earlier reference, it was noted that an improvement procedure would be implemented subsequently. In this case study, the tabu search mechanism has proven to be so efficient that even fairly poor initial solutions can be improved into solutions which are comparable to those based on good initial solutions (See Table 4.4). All the details of these improved routing solutions can be found in Appendix E.

Table 4.4 Improved Solutions

Table 4.4.1 Improved Solutions by Heuristics Based on Nearest Neighbor Insertion

No.	1	2	3	4	5	6	7	8	9	10	11	12	Average
Pickup Time Deviation/min	15.1	23.6	30.6	46.4	59.5	64.1	74.5	88.4	94.7	107.6	111.5	123.9	
Taxi Used	9	7	6	5	4	5	4	5	3	4	4	5	5.08
Total Travel Cost/min	282.8	279.4	288.0	279.9	295.5	269.1	277.9	267.7	280.9	288.3	306.8	293.4	284.2

Table 4. 4. 2 Improved Solutions by Heuristics Based on Sweep Insertion

No.	1	2	3	4	5	6	7	8	9	10	11	12	Average
Pickup Time Deviation/min	15. 1	23. 6	30. 6	46. 4	59. 5	64. 1	74. 5	88. 4	94. 7	107. 6	111. 5	123. 9	
Taxi Used	9	7	6	5	4	5	4	5	3	4	5	4	5. 08
Total Travel Cost/min	273. 5	285. 3	286. 9	279. 0	279. 7	281. 9	308. 2	288. 8	282. 5	285. 1	288. 7	296. 1	286. 3

Table 4. 4. 3 Improved Solutions by Heuristics Based on Earliest Time Insertion

No.	1	2	3	4	5	6	7	8	9	10	11	12	Average
Pickup Time Deviation/min	15. 1	23. 6	30. 6	46. 4	59. 5	64. 1	74. 5	88. 4	94. 7	107. 6	111. 5	123. 9	
Taxi Used	9	7	6	5	4	5	4	5	3	4	4	4	5. 0
Total Travel Cost/min	267. 2	275. 4	283. 3	283. 0	288. 0	279. 0	274. 6	293. 2	286. 6	294. 6	292. 1	300. 4	284. 8

On the whole, the larger the booking time deviation, the fewer were the taxis required. However, the deviation defined as $\sum_{i=1}^{n} \mid T_i - \overline{T} \mid /n$ only indicated the average deviation from the average booking time, and a large value of deviation did not necessarily mean that the booking demands were almost evenly distributed along the time space that could guarantee obtaining a solution in which fewer taxis were involved.

The proposed earliest time window insertion algorithm could generate a good initial solution efficiently in that fewer taxis were required, compared with the initial solutions based on the other two heuristics. In addition, this initial solution was not improved significantly within a limited computation time (See Figure 4. 1). Hence, for an online service with a strict time constraint, this initial solution could even be adopted as a sensible solution where the improvement phase was omitted so as to entertain customers more quickly without losing too much solution quality. Through the customized two-phase method, a practical routing plan for a batch of booking demands could be generated quickly around five seconds to provide on-line decisions. The comparisons of experimental results between the proposed system

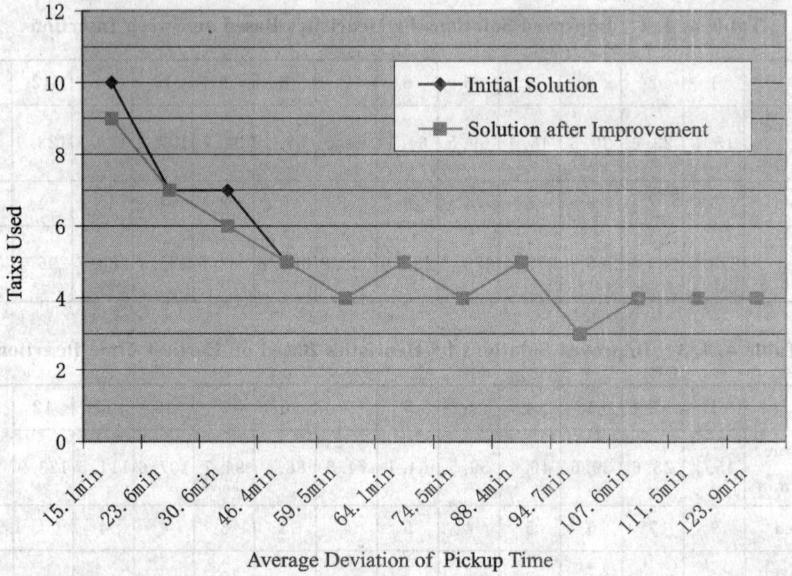

Figure 4. 1 Experimental Results Based on Earliest Time Insertion Heuristics

and the existing one are shown in Table 4. 5.

Table 4. 5 Comparisons between the Existing System and the Proposed System

Number of Booking Request	Average Number of Taxi Involved under the Existing System	Average Number of Taxi Involved under the Proposed System	Improvement in terms of vehicle number/(%)
40	40	5. 0	87. 5

In Singapore, all the taxis running around the road network would receive advance booking information and qualify to bid for the booking job, regardless of whether they were occupied at that moment. Note that one of the main features for the advance booking service is that the booking request should be made at least 30 minutes earlier than the pickup time. Therefore, it is usually possible for those occupied taxis to release theirs passengers within 30 minutes in a small island like Singapore. Hence, with the overwhelmingly higher number of available taxis against the number of advance booking demands within certain time intervals, such as 40 requests within every five minutes, in the worst case scenario, it can be assumed that no taxi can be fortunate enough to bid successfully for more than one booking job during the same time interval (actually, it is in reality a reasonable assumption). Thus with each batch of an average 40 demands within five minutes, 40 different taxis will be assigned to serve those demands, compared to the average number of taxis generated by the proposed system. In fact, the average improvement is as high as 87.5% (See Table 4.5).

4.6 SUMMARY

In this chapter, the potential employment of a new taxi dispatch system modeled after a customized PDPTW problem was identified and explored. A two-phase method was adopted and an earliest time window insertion algorithm to efficiently generate the initial solution for this 'ad hoc' problem was also proposed. Experimental results show the efficiency of the proposed taxi dispatching system.

Although this study was motivated by a practical problem faced by taxi operators in Singapore and did not intend to make a contribution with regard to the algorithm initially, it did raise the STAR problem, which is a special version of the normal PDPTW, discussed its characteristics and requirements, and proposed a particular construction method to better solve this 'ad hoc' problem.

The main contribution of this study is that a revolutionary new system was proposed for a real life problem of taxi advance booking in Singapore, which would reduce operating costs, reduce empty cruising time, and could be deployed by taxi companies directly without any extra physical devices or facilities.

Under the proposed system, the benefits for taxi drivers, taxi companies and customers, are summarized as follows:

1. For Taxi Drivers

There will be an increase in productivity since drivers can take more bookings with less empty cruising, thus reducing operating costs. The system might also increase taxi drivers' incomes because they are able to accept more bookings with extra surcharges.

2. For Taxi Companies

The most attractive part is that an increase in efficiency and resource utilization would be expected. With the same resources, taxi companies will be able to handle a higher throughput of bookings. In other words, with the same demand level, a taxi company could reduce the number of vehicles in use as well as the number of drivers. Therefore, the costs for the company could be reduced.

More importantly perhaps, the taxi drivers will be more willing to accept a packaged advance booking rather than a single current booking, because of the booking surcharges that would be multiplied by the number of trips. To influence the booking behavior (that indirectly minimizes the operating cost), the taxi company could re-set the surcharges of the booking service, so that the surcharge of the advance booking becomes lower than the current booking (currently in Singapore, the surcharge of the advance booking is higher than that of the current booking). This would again encourage customers to use advance bookings rather than wait until the last minute to make a current booking. If the population of customers who use advance bookings is large enough, the taxi company could take advantage of this result to arrange the taxi fleet in a systematic manner, resulting in reduced fleet size and operating costs. Consequently, the advance booking service might be given a further boost because of the discounted final taxi fare, which could be even lower than the street hailing price in future.

3. For Customers

With the reduced surcharge for advance bookings, customers may be more willing to make bookings in advance rather than make current bookings in a hurry or wait for taxis at taxi stands (or by the roadside).

CHAPTER 5
USERS' RESPONSE TOWARDS EXISTING TAXI BOOKING SERVICES

5.1 INTRODUCTION

The proposals presented in Chapters 3 and 4 have been submitted to two major taxi companies (Comfort Taxis and CityCab) and Land Transport Authority in Singapore. Based on feedbacks from these taxi operators and policy maker, a survey from users' viewpoint towards the existing taxi booking services was conducted, to help the taxi operators and policy makers to gain insights on users' expectation and behavior.

The objective of this survey was to further validate the value and feasibility of the proposed dispatch strategies in real life. In light of this objective, a survey questionnaire was designed to poll the opinion from the population of study, on the subject of users' booking behavior, taxi arrival time, booking surcharge structure and other related concerns. After consolidating these necessary information and knowledge, proper survey design techniques were adopted to ensure the best accuracy in response. Then, a survey with a size of 600 respondents was carried out and their responses gathered and analyzed.

5.2 MOTIVATION AND OBJECTIVE

The proposed dispatch strategies in Chapter 3 and especially in Chapter 4 will significantly change the overall picture of local taxi operations (taxi fleet management, fare structure and related users' behaviors etc.), and to some extent, may even revamp the traditional concepts of taxi services (including taxi booking and street hailing) known to the players and users in Singapore. A survey from users' perspective was therefore motivated to convince market leader and players before all these transformations come into practice. The objective of this survey aims at justifying the value and feasibility of those proposals, by seeking answers to the following two issues.

1. The value to further reduce taxi arrival time

This is an issue related to current-booking services. Under the existing dispatch system, the taxi assigned to a current-booking job can reach the customer within 10-15 on average (data provided by the largest taxi company in Singapore). Is it necessary to further reduce the taxi arrival time? In other words, how long is the 'ideal' time interval to reach the customer? Is it always the shorter/sooner the better?

There are many users who prefer to do bookings at their offices/homes where these locations are often more convenient and comfortable. Because of the walking distance between offices/homes and the pick up locations, the taxi arrival times are certainly not the sooner the better for this group of users. Instead they would rather perform other tasks and have the taxi wait for them when they reach the pickup locations. If the aforementioned users' booking behavior forms the majority, it does not make sense to further reduce the arrival time at present. In other words, the strategy proposed in Chapter 3 does not have too much value in the real world.

2. The feasibility of trip chaining strategy

Currently, the volume of advance booking is too few compared with that of current booking. In fact, advance booking contributes a mere three to four percent of the total booking volume (based on the data provided by the local taxi companies). Moreover, in contrast to the diverse pickup/destination locations of current-booking demands, advance bookings are often concentrated on some origins or destinations (such as airport) rather than randomly generated data sets in Chapter 4 Consequently, is it worth paying attention to such a small group? Perhaps more importantly, due to concentrated demands at specific locations and relatively few bookings over time, it would be impossible to chain as many calls as the system might wish. Then, the proposed trip chaining strategy is of little value to the taxi companies, nor practical. To clear those doubts, it is necessary to investigate whether the existing pattern (or user behavior) of advance booking service are inherent characteristics of the service itself or are actually affected by the external circumstance such as the prevailing fare structure.

5.3 CHOOSING SURVEY METHOD

According to Cartor and Williamson (1996), a sample survey is to obtain information from a few respondents in order to describe the characteristics of the entire population. Survey is the answer under certain circumstances in sampling the population when it is too large to be handled in any other way.

There are generally three main methods: mail survey, phone survey, and personal survey (Salant and Dillman 1994). Mail survey is the most popular as well as the cheapest survey method, which always uses a questionnaire. But it suffers from a poor response rate (usually between 10 and 50 percent). Phone survey normally gets quite a high response rate (about 70 percent), but is slightly more expensive than a mail survey due to the telephone charges incurred and the cost of qualified personnel to ask the questions. Personal survey is effective in winning a respondent's trust, though it is no doubt the most costly of the three survey methods. To ensure a high response rate and accurate results within a relatively short response time, personal surveys at multiple selected locations was chosen as the survey method for this study.

The survey was carried out with 600 respondents, at different locations in Singapore, including Ngee Ann city, Lucky Plaza, Suntec City, Parco Bugis Junction and City Hall, which are among the most popular locations within CBD in terms of origins of taxi trips.

5.4 SURVEY CONSTRUCTION AND FORMAT

It is necessary to have a reasonable understanding and knowledge of the problem domain (taxi services) in order to set up the survey questions accurately so as to obtain responses that are reliable, genuine and will help in the areas of study. In other words, the survey questions must be effectively constructed towards the desired objective and scope. The survey questions must also be drafted in such a way that non-sampling errors are minimized (Charles & Gerald 1981).

In order to draft the questions, the following important points were noted (David 1998):

ⅰ. The questions must be relevant and important to the objectives and scope of the study.

ⅱ. The meaning of the questions must be unambiguous and have no wording problems.

ⅲ. The response to the questions can be analyzed statistically.

ⅳ. The questions will uncover variability in answers from the population.

The first and second points are very obvious. To satisfy the third and fourth points, close-ended multiple-choice questions were adopted for most questions instead of open-ended questions. This is because it is very difficult to carry out statistical analysis on open-ended questions due to the variability in the answers that will be provided by the respondents (Saw 1990). There are however a few open-ended questions in the survey questionnaire of this project to encourage response. The opinions provided by the respondents will not be analyzed statistically. Close-ended multiple-choice questions enable uniformity and comparability in the answers provided by respondents which makes it easy for data processing (Saw 1990). Close-ended multiple-choice questions also offer more variability in response which facilitate statistical analysis as compared to close-ended dichotomous questions which respondents only answer either yes or no (Saw 1990).

After considering all the four points, the survey questions were drafted. The survey form is separated into two parts. The first part determines the demographic data of the respondents. The second part is the actual questionnaire itself to determine the users' response towards local taxi booking services. The entire survey questionnaire consists of two pages and takes about three minutes to complete.

Some preparatory work had been done before the survey was carried out so as to ensure it a success. In order to discover pitfalls in the questions that would result in undesired responses, comments from both sides of users and service providers have been sought to pre-test the survey questionnaire. The piloting questions were first tested on a sample of 10 respondents randomly selected from regular taxi users on university campus. Meanwhile correspondences with local taxi companies had been made to seek their opinions and remarks on the preliminary survey form. Modifications were subsequently made based on the suggestions given by the individual respondents and taxi operators. The pilot survey was then developed into the final version of the questionnaire that is more comprehensive, clear and unbiased. The final survey questionnaire and results can be found in Appendix F and Appendix G.

5.5 COMMENTS ON THE SURVEY QUESTIONS

This section discusses the reasons behind the questions in the survey.

1. Demographics

The sex of the respondents is to carry out a hypothesis test to see whether there is a significant difference in the survey response between the sexes.

The age of the respondents is required for the author to analyse the distribution of responses based on their ages. Six different age groups were considered in this survey.

The income level of the respondents is to test whether there is a significant difference in the responses between the income groups. Five income levels were considered in this survey.

2. Main questionnaire

Q1. This question determines the frequency of the respondent in using the taxi service, i. e. , the answer determines whether he/she is a frequent/regular user or only an occasional user.

Q2. This question determines the frequency that the respondent uses the taxi booking service, i. e. , determine whether he/she frequently/regularly uses taxi booking service, or only uses it occasionally. If the respondent never uses booking service, then he/she will skip to answer Question 5 directly.

Q3. This question finds out the reason why the respondent uses taxi booking service. This will help taxi operators to gain insight into the existing taxi booking services from users' perspective and to design/upgrade the service accordingly.

Q4. This question determines the location that the respondent usually makes taxi booking. The respondent who selects 'at office/home' will be asked to answer additional Questions Q4. a to Q4. c. Q4. a finds out the reasons why these respondents book taxis at offices/homes. Q4. b finds out these respondents estimated taxi arrival time. Q4. c finds out whether these respondents would like to adjust their booking behavior when current conditions of the booking services are changed.

Q5. This question determines whether the fare structure will affect users' choices. The question is divided into two parts, Q5. a and Q5. b. The first part aims to find out the proportion of respondents who are willing to shift to make use of advance-booking service when the advance-booking fee is cheaper than the current-booking fee. The second part finds out the proportion of respondents who are willing to shift to advance-booking service when booking a taxi in advance is even cheaper than hailing a taxi at the roadside.

5. 6 SURVEY RESULTS AND ANALYSIS

In this section, the results of the survey will be presented and discussed. The first part shows the demographics of the respondents. The second part presents the detailed results of main questions in this survey. The third part presents the analysis in terms of hypothesis testing using non-parametric methods.

1. Survey sampling results

The distributions of samples are summarized in Figures 5. 1 to 5. 3, which illustrate the distribution of respondents by sex, age and income respectively. The numbers of respondents are indicated accordingly in the charts.

2. Analysis of survey results

In this part, analysis of the survey responses will be presented. Appendix *G* can be referred for more details.

First, the survey results of questions 1 to 3 are summarized in Figures 5. 4 to 5. 6. It can be observed from Figure 5. 4 that more than half of the survey respondents are frequent and regular taxi users, who use taxi service at least three times in a week. However, 45. 8% of those respondents only use taxi service less than two times per week.

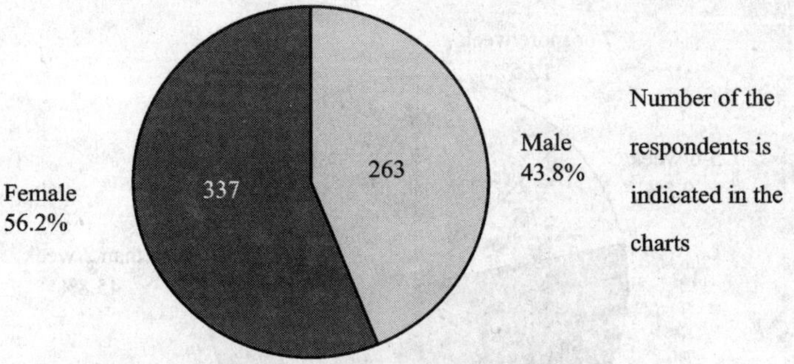

Figure 5. 1 Distribution of Respondents by Sex

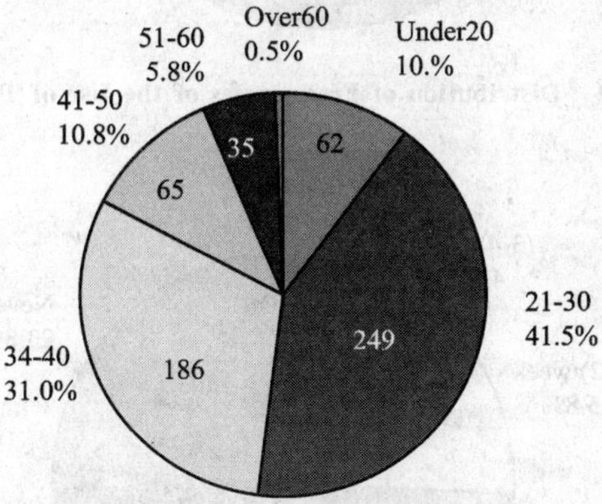

Figure 5. 2 Distribution of Respondents by Age

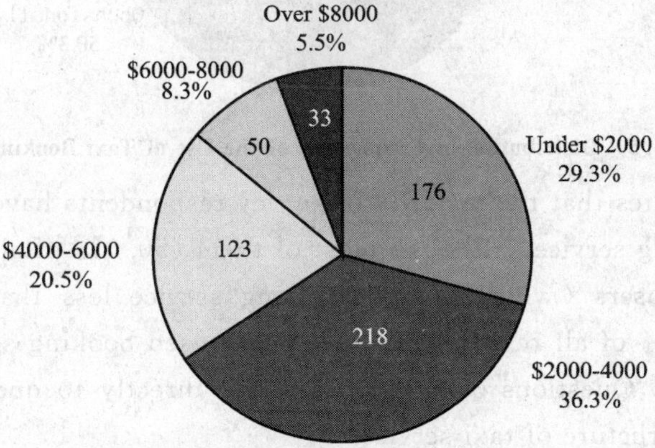

Figure 5. 3 Distribution of Respondents by Family Monthly Income

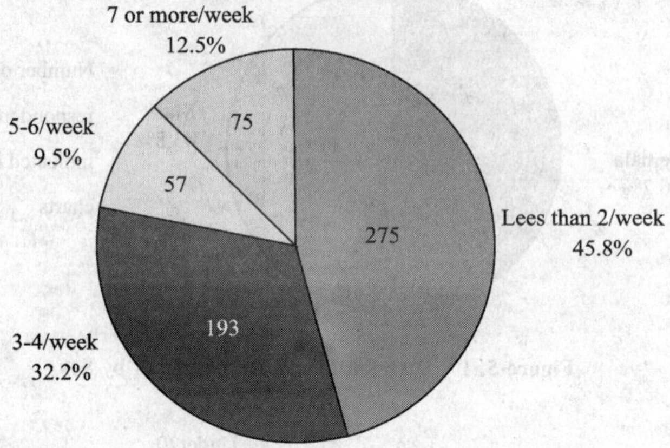

Figure 5.4 Distribution of Frequencies of the Use of Taxi Services

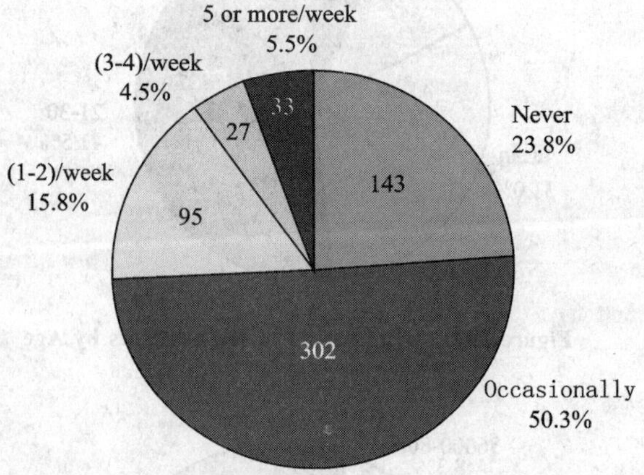

Figure 5.5 Distribution of Frequencies of the Use of Taxi Booking Services

Figure 5.5 indicates that the majority of survey respondents have the experience of using taxi booking service, although most of them (50.3% of all respondents) are only occasional users (who use taxi booking service less than once a week). Moreover, 23.8% of all respondents have never used booking service. They were requested to skip Questions 3 and 4, and went directly to question 5, which is related to fare structure of taxi service.

Figure 5.6 lists different motives for which respondents use booking services. Majority of the respondents use booking services actually because they cannot find a taxi at the roadside, and hence switch to seek help from the booking system. That is followed by the second incentive, which is to guarantee that he/she will get a taxi at a particular time, for instance, for a trip to the airport in the early morning. The third reason is to save time from queuing at taxi stands. Only a few respondents book a taxi because of brand loyalty. These results are useful for taxi operators to design and improve booking service in future.

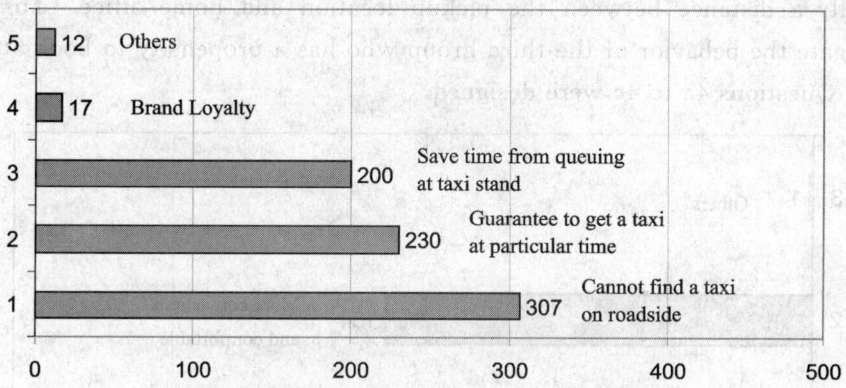

Figure 5.6 Motives of Using Taxi Booking Services

Questions 4 and 5 are the core part of this survey. Figures 5.7 to 5.11 illustrate the results obtained.

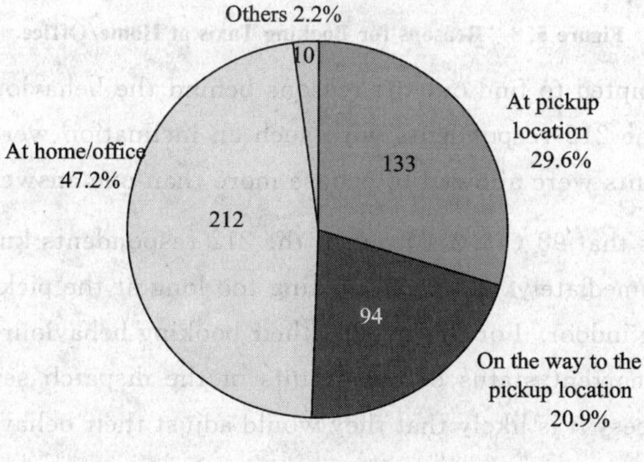

Figure 5.7 Locations of Taxi Booking

Question 4 only looked into respondents who have experience with current-booking service (212 respondents in this study). Of these respondents, 29.6% of them make bookings at their pickup locations, 20.9% of them called for a taxi on the ways to the pickup locations, and 47.2% of them usually make the bookings at their homes/offices. For the first and second groups (which book right at the pickup locations and on the ways to pickup locations), it is reasonable to assume that they wish taxis to arrive immediately (or as soon as possible). Nevertheless, respondents in the third group may not wish taxis to appear too fast, since there is generally a distance between the pickup location and home/office. To further investigate the behavior of the third group who has a propensity to book at home/office, Questions 4a to 4c were designed.

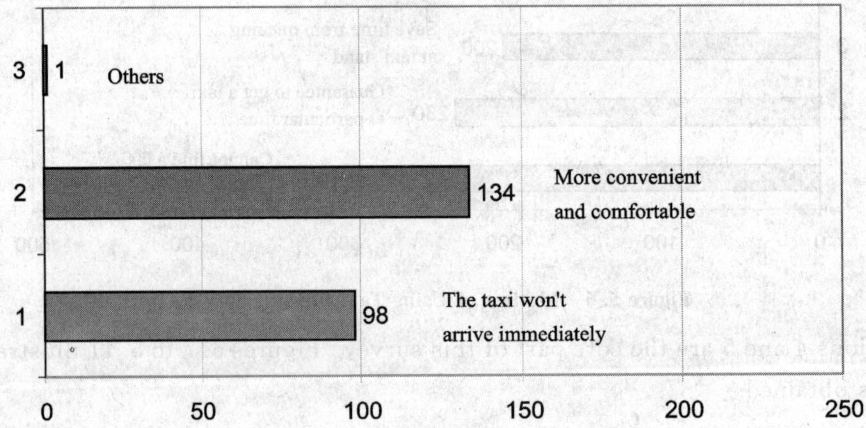

Figure 5.8 Reasons for Booking Taxis at Home/Office

Question 4a attempted to find out the reasons behind the behaviour of 'booking at home/office'. The 212 respondents with such an inclination were asked Question 4a, and respondents were allowed to choose more than one answer.

Figure 5.8 shows that 98 (46.2%) out of the 212 respondents know that the taxis will not arrive immediately. To avoid waiting too long at the pickup location, they make the booking indoor. For this group, their booking behaviour is to some extent nurtured by the current status or constraints of the dispatch service. When taxi arrival time reduces, it is likely that they would adjust their behaviour to follow the new conditions.

On the other hand, 134 (63.2%) out of 212 respondents feel more convenient and comfortable to book at their offices/homes. It can be observed that there are respondents who tick both reasons of sluggish arrival time and indoor convenience/comforts. Those who are only concern about indoor convenience/comforts, are less likely to expect a taxi to arrive early.

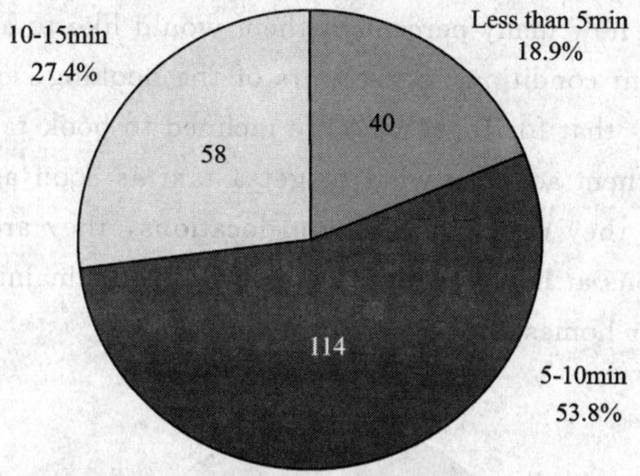

Figure 5. 9 Users' Estimated Taxi Arrival Time

Question 4b was designed to investigate how long is a user's estimation of taxi arrival time when he/she makes a current booking. Figure 5. 9 shows that 18. 9% of them book a taxi less than 5 minutes earlier. However, the majority (53. 8%) of them call for a taxi 5-10 minutes in advance. Moreover, 27. 4% of them can even tolerate 10-15 minutes for a taxi requested via current-booking service.

The survey can be used to examine whether the respondents have the potential to switch to use advance-booking service. For the group of customers who often book a taxi before a relatively long period, they actually know of the time they would need a taxi. Hence they can take this advantage to book a taxi beforehand, to compensate the waiting time. Therefore, if advance-booking service is cheaper, they are very likely to use advance booking since they have planned their trips in advance.

As mentioned at the beginning of this book, the minimum time requirement to make an advance booking is 30 minutes earlier. Thus, it is very likely that there are a group of users who purposely make a booking within 30 minutes even for a well-planned trip (a trip which is confirmed more than half an hour ahead of time), in order to avoid higher advance-booking fee. This group of users is very likely to shift to use advance-booking service when the surcharge of advance booking is cheaper.

Question 4c aims at finding out among those respondents who prefer to book at their homes/offices, how many percent of them would like to adjust their booking behavior when current conditions/constraints of the booking services are changed. Figure 5.10 indicates that for those who are inclined to book taxis at their homes/offices, 52.8% of them actually wish to get a taxi as soon as possible. If taxis always arrive before they reach their pickup locations, they are willing to change their booking locations at homes/offices. However, the remaining 45.8% will still stick to book at their homes/offices.

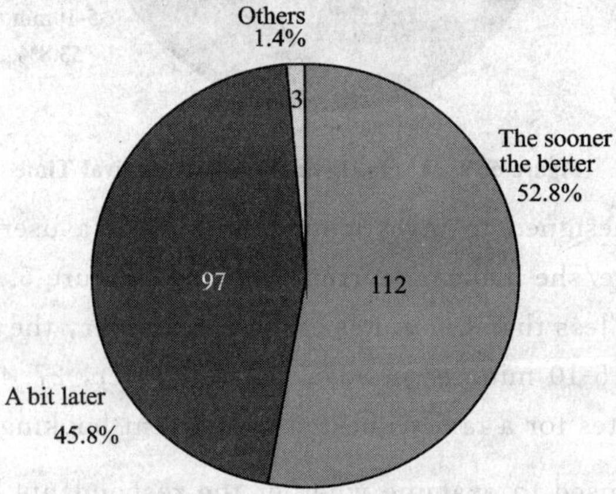

Figure 5.10 Users' Desired Taxi Arrival Time

An important conclusion can be drawn here, since even within those people who book at homes/offices, more than half of them wish to obtain a taxi immediately. On the whole, including users who book right at the pickup locations and on the ways to the pickup locations, 75.3% of the total respondents who make current booking actually wish to have a taxi to serve them as soon as possible. In other words, the majority of current-booking users will benefit from a system that dispatches taxi using real-time traffic conditions. Hence, the value of proposed real-time dispatch strategy to reduce taxi arrival time appears valid.

Questions 5a and 5b were designed for all respondents involved in this survey. Figure 5.11 points out that 75.3% of all respondents are willing to shift from

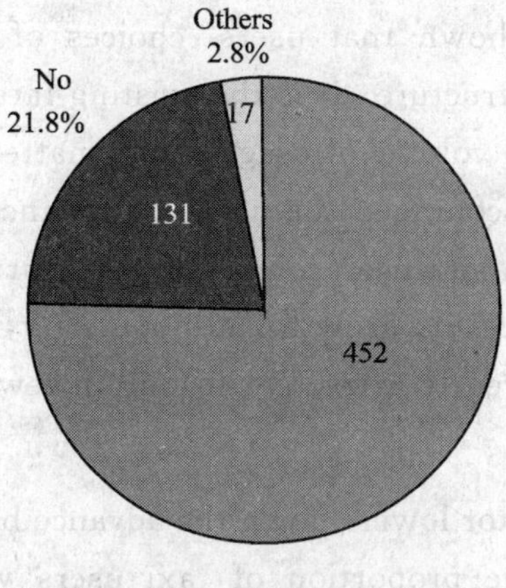

Figure 5. 11 Distribution of Users Willing to Shift to Advance-Booking Service when Advance-Booking Service is Cheaper than Current-Booking Service

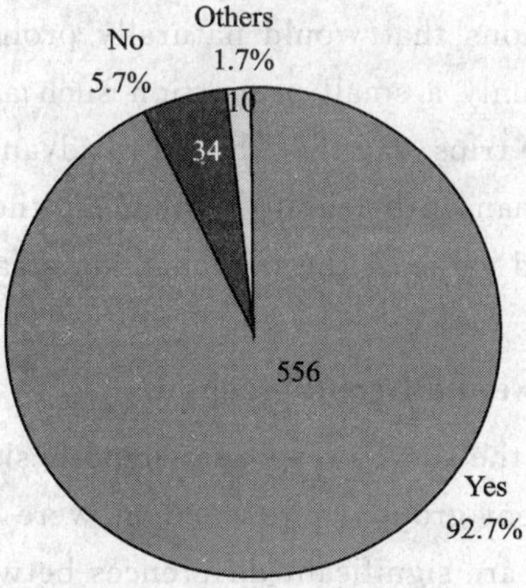

Figure 5. 12 Distribution of Users Willing to Shift to Advance-Booking Service when Advance-Booking Service is Cheaper than Street Hailing

current-booking service to advance-booking service when the later is cheaper than the earlier. Figure 5. 12 shows that 92. 7% of all respondents are willing to use advance-booking service as much as possible when advance-booking service is cheaper than street hailing. Of course, to use advance-booking service successfully, a user must be capable of planning his/her trips in advance. However, even for a small portion of users, for example, either 10% of current-booking service user or 5% of the street-hailing user who can successfully shift to advance booking service, there will be sufficient demand for trip chaining for advance bookings.

The results have evidently shown that users' choices of using taxi service are actually sensitive to the fare structure. It is the existing fare structure that governs users' behavior and affects the volume of usage. As a matter of fact, the prevailing fare structure has strongly discouraged the usage of advance booking service. The high price of booking a taxi in advance (compared with current booking and street hailing, see Table 2.1) restricts its growth and popularity, which is also the main reason that the service is currently attractive to only a few types of trips such as trips to the airport.

If the market leader and operator lowers down the advance booking fee, as indicated in the survey results, a large proportion of taxi users would like to seek the possibility of using advance-booking service when they need a taxi. As a result, the real world demand for advance bookings will no longer be too few or too concentrated on some locations that would naturally prohibit the chance to chain those trips. Actually with only a small proportion such as 5% of total daily taxi trips, approximately 50,000 trips/day that shifted to advance bookings, the volume of demands will be more than sufficient to implement the proposed trip-chaining strategy. The feasibility and value of the trip chaining strategy have been justified by the survey results.

3. Analysis of responses between different groups

To complete the analysis of the survey response, hypothesis tests on the differences in responses between different groups of respondent were carried out. The motive was to check whether there are significant differences between the responses based on the demographic data. In this study, sex and income were examined. As Questions 4 and 5 are the core part of this survey, those results were hence scrutinized in hypothesis tests, where non-parametric methods were adopted.

1) Test 1

Step 1. Null hypothesis H_{S0}: No difference in booking behavior between sexes.

Alternative hypothesis H_{S1}: Respondents' sex affects their booking behavior.

Step 2. Level of Significance: $\alpha=0.05$

Step 3. Criterion: Reject the null hypothesis if χ^2 larger than the value $\chi^2_{0.05}$ for degrees of freedom defined as $(r-1)(c-1)$, where r is the number of rows and c is the number of columns in the contingency table; and χ^2 is given by

$$\chi^2 = \sum_{i=1}^{r} \sum_{j=1}^{c} \frac{(o_{ij} - e_{ij})^2}{e_{ij}}$$

Step 4. Calculation: the details can be found in Tables 5.1 to 5.3.

Table 5.1 Contingency Tables of Different Gender for Question 4

Answer	1	2	3	4	Total	
Male	52	55	80	5	192	Observed
Female	81	39	132	5	257	
Total	133	94	212	10	449	

Answer	1	2	3	4	Total	
Male	56.87	40.2	90.655	4.3	192	Expected
Female	76.13	53.8	121.3	5.7	257	
Total	133	94	212	10	449	

DOF	3	
$\chi^2_{0.05,3}$	7.815	
χ^2	12.645	Reject

Table 5.2 Contingency Tables of Different Gender for Question 5a

Answer	1	2	3	Total	
Male	188	68	7	263	Observed
Female	264	63	10	337	
Total	452	131	17	600	

Answer	1	2	3	Total	
Male	198.1	57.4	7.45	263	Expected
Female	253.9	73.6	9.55	337	
Total	452	131	17	600	

DOF	2	
$\chi^2_{0.05,2}$	5.991	
χ^2	4.415	Do not reject

Table 5.3 Contingency Tables of Different Gender for Question 5b

Answer	1	2	3	Total	
Male	244	15	4	263	Observed
Female	312	19	6	337	
Total	556	34	10	600	

Answer	1	2	3	Total	
Male	243.7	14.9	4.383	263	Expected
Female	312.3	19.1	5.617	337	
Total	556	34	10	600	

DOF	2	
$\chi^2_{0.05,2}$	5.991	
χ^2	0.061	Do not reject

Step 5. Decision: From Table 5.1, H_{S0} is rejected at $\alpha=0.05$ for Question 4, as the χ^2 value is 12.645 (less than 7.815). We can conclude that women behave differently than men in their way in booking a taxi. It can also be observed that more women than men, have a tendency to book at home/office.

From Tables 5.2-5.3, H_{S0} is not rejected at $\alpha=0.05$ for Questions 5a and 5b in which the χ^2 values are both less than the criteria (less than 5.991). Hence, we can conclude that there is no difference between men and women for their responses to taxi service price structure.

2) Test 2

Step 1. Null hypothesis H_{I0}: No difference in booking behavior between incomes.

Alternative hypothesis H_{I1}: Respondents' income affects their booking behavior.

Step 2. Level of Significance: $\alpha=0.05$

Step 3. Criterion: Reject the null hypothesis if χ^2 larger than the value $\chi^2_{0.05}$ for degrees of freedom defined as $(r-1)(c-1)$, where r is the number of rows and c is the number of columns in the contingency table; and χ^2 is given by

$$\chi^2 = \sum_{i=q}^{r} \sum_{j=1}^{c} \frac{(o_{ij} - e_{ij})^2}{e_{ij}}$$

Step 4. Calculation: the details can be found in Tables 5.4 to 5.6.

Table 5.4 Contingency Tables of Different Income for Question 4

Answer	1	2	3	4	Total	
Income level 1	30	20	48	5	103	Observed
Income level 2	50	46	71	5	172	
Income level 3	26	16	62	0	104	
Income level 4	13	7	21	0	41	
Income level 5	14	5	10	0	29	
Total	133	94	212	10	449	

Answer	1	2	3	4	Total	
Income level 1	30.51	21.56	48.63	2.294	103	Expected
Income level 2	50.95	36.01	81.21	3.8307	172	
Income level 3	30.81	21.77	49.1	2.3163	104	
Income level 4	12.14	8.584	19.36	0.9131	41	
Income level 5	8.59	6.071	13.69	0.6459	29	
Total	133	94	212	10	449	

DOF	12	
$\chi^2_{0.05,12}$	21.026	
χ^2	22.379	Reject

Table 5.5 Contingency Tables of Different Income for Question 5a

Answer	1	2	3	Total	
Income level 1	128	42	6	176	Observed
Income level 2	164	46	8	218	
Income level 3	99	23	1	123	
Income level 4	42	8	0	50	
Income level 5	19	12	2	33	
Total	452	131	17	600	

Table 5.5 (Continued)

Answer	1	2	3	Total	
Income level 1	132.59	38	4.9867	176	Expected
Income level 2	164.23	48	6.1767	218	
Income level 3	92.66	27	3.485	123	
Income level 4	37.667	11	1.4167	50	
Income level 5	24.86	7.2	0.935	33	
Total	452	131	17	600	

DOF	8	
$\chi^2_{0.05,8}$	15.507	
χ^2	12.527	Do not reject

Table 5.6 Contingency Tables of Different Income for Question 5b

Answer	1	2	3	Total	
Income level 1	162	9	5	176	Observed
Income level 2	204	11	3	218	
Income level 3	118	4	1	123	
Income level 4	45	4	1	50	
Income level 5	27	6	0	33	
Total	556	34	10	600	

Answer	1	2	3	Total	
Income level 1	163.09	9.97	2.93333	176	Expected
Income level 2	202.01	12.4	3.63333	218	
Income level 3	113.98	6.97	2.05	123	
Income level 4	46.333	2.83	0.83333	50	
Income level 5	30.58	1.87	0.55	33	
Total	556	34	10	600	

DOF	8	
$\chi^2_{0.05,8}$	15.507	
χ^2	14.422	Do not reject

Step 5. Decision: From Table 5.4, H_{I0} is rejected at $\alpha=0.05$ for Question 4 where the χ^2 value is 22.379 (larger than 21.026). It can be seen that different income levels affect users' booking habits.

From Table 5.5-5.6, H_{I0} is not rejected at $\alpha=0.05$ for Question 5a and 5b in which the χ^2 values are both less than the criteria 15.507. To taxi service price structure, we can say that there is no difference of responses between people with different income.

5.7 SUMMARY OF SURVEY

The chapter has provided an insight on how taxi users feel about issues related to taxi booking services. This basic understanding on users behavior is very important to the taxi operators as well as policy makers in terms of considerations for service upgrading and fare restructuring. The survey confirms that the proposed dispatch strategies for current booking and advance booking are in reality valuable and feasible.

Based on the survey results, more than 75.5% of the respondents who use current booking service want or expect taxi to arrive as soon as possible. If the advance-booking fee is cheaper than the current booking fee, 75.3% of the respondents are willing to shift to use advance booking service, on the condition that they are able to plan their trip in advance. The survey results also indicate that when advance-booking service is cheaper than street hailing, 92.7% of the respondents are willing to obtain a taxi through advance booking as long as they can plan the trips earlier. The survey results in general are strongly supportive of the strategies proposed in Chapters 3 and 4. The survey results generated can also serve as a basis for any further recommendations made to taxi operators and related policy makers as well as useful information for future research.

CHAPTER 6
CONCLUSIONS

6.1 CONCLUSIONS

This study aims at improving taxi dispatch services using real-time traffic and customer information. First, an overview of previous work in urban taxi modeling and current status of taxi booking/dispatching operations in Singapore has been made. Subsequently, innovative taxi dispatch strategies were proposed, for both current and advance-booking services. A microscopic simulation model was adopted to represent the taxi movements under different dispatch systems with realistic background traffic. The simulation model was used as a test bed for this study and the usefulness of the proposed dispatch strategies evaluated. Suitable MOEs (Measures of Effectiveness), which include travel times, travel distances and number of taxis involved, were used to measure the impact of new dispatch strategies. To further validate the feasibility and acceptance of the proposed strategies in real life, a survey from users' point of view was carried out with a sample size of 600 respondents. The main conclusions derived are highlighted as follows:

i. In contrast to the existing taxi dispatch system that handles current-bookings based on the shortest, straight-line distance to the customer location, an alternative dispatch system was proposed, whereby the dispatch of taxis is determined by real-time traffic conditions with the shortest-time path. Results of the simulations show that the proposed dispatch system is capable of dispatching taxis more quickly to reach customers; leading to more than 50% reductions in passenger pick up time and average travel distance. Hence it may result in higher standards of customer service, and a fairer taxi assignment to better meet customer demands.

ⅱ. A novel trip-chaining strategy for taxi advance booking based on a customized algorithm of Pickup and Delivery Problem with Time Window (PDPTW) problem has been proposed. The idea is to chain several bookings with demand time points which are spread out within a reasonable period of time, and with each pick-up point coinciding with or being within close proximity to the previous drop-off location. Based on the simulation results, the proposed system for taxi advance bookings would reduce the taxi fleet size by up to 87.5%, in serving the same level of advance booking demands. This will not only result in more reasonable fare structures for taxi companies to encourage users to book taxis in advance and discourage last-minute requests, but also bring benefits to customers, drivers and taxi companies in terms of enjoying a high level of service with low price, increasing productivity with less empty cruising and increasing resource utilization. Thus, the trip-chaining strategy proposed has the potential to change the concept of the taxi booking service currently operating in Singapore.

ⅲ. Based on the survey results, more than 75.5% of the respondents who use current booking service want or expect taxis to arrive as soon as possible.

ⅳ. The survey results has shown that if the advance-booking fee is cheaper than the current-booking fee, 75.3% of the respondents are willing to shift to use advance-booking service, on the condition that they are able to plan their trip in advance.

ⅴ. The survey results also indicate that when advance-booking service is cheaper than street hailing, 92.7% of the respondents are willing to obtain a taxi through advance booking as long as they can plan the trips earlier.

6.2 RESEARCH CONTRIBUTIONS

The main contributions of this study can be described as follows:

ⅰ. A comprehensive literature review on the modeling of urban taxi service has been made and the details of the operation of the local taxi booking service have been documented, which can serve as a stepping-stone for future researches in the field of both analytical modeling and practical application of urban taxi operations.

ⅱ. A survey with a size of 600 respondents has been carried out, to investigate users' response towards the existing taxi booking system. The opinions regarding the users' booking behavior, taxi arrival time and booking fee structure have been polled from the population of study. The survey results have not only justified the strategies proposed in this book, but will also benefit operators, researchers and policy makers in their future R&D efforts.

ⅲ. The proposed dispatch systems based on link-to-link shortest-time path would reduce more than 50% in passenger pick-up time and average travel distance to meet current-booking demand. In fact, one of the local taxi operators has been developing a new dispatch system for booking services, that is a step close to our proposed system. The abovementioned vehicle dispatch algorithm for current bookings is trying to incorporate the static/historical travel time of each street link section.

ⅳ. The proposed system for taxi advance bookings could reduce the taxi fleet size by up to 87.5%, in serving the same level of advance-booking demand. To substantiate the implementation, the existing taxi companies are suggested to setup a special fleet only to cater for the advance-booking requests so as to reduce operating cost in terms of capital, overhead and maintenance. Whilst for new players who plan to enter the market, they may adopt the trip-chaining strategy to mainly focusing on the advance booking services, not only to distinguish themselves from the existing competitors, but also get more profits via operating a smaller fleet size to serve a larger number of advance-booking trips and maintaining a high service level.

ⅴ. In the aspect of theoretical contribution, the Singapore Taxi Advance Reservations (STAR) problem was introduced in the book, which was based on a real-life problem faced by taxi operators in Singapore. In fact it is a special version of the PDPTW. The STAR problem's characteristics and requirements were discussed, and a particular construction method to better solve this ad hoc' problem was also proposed and tested.

ⅵ. The research will help the market leaders or related policy makers to steer the taxi market onto the right track of quality, convenience and efficiency, especially in cities where taxi is one of the important transportation modes. It is expected that this study will not only change the current fare structure of taxi services, but will also revamp the traditional concept of taxi services/operations in Singapore. From economics point of view, a customer should pay more if he/she requests the service immediately in an arbitrary/irregular manner, such as street hailing and last minute booking. Other regular customers or cooperative customers who inform the service provider in advance should pay less, such as advance-booking users who plan their trips and inform the taxi company at least half an hour earlier. Adjusting the fare structure will certainly increase the usage of advance booking as indicated in the survey results. Under an ideal situation, if all the taxi demands are manageable or systematically arranged, a taxi may only run out onto the street network when it is pulled by a confirmed demand, or stays in the car park otherwise, hence avoiding empty cruising and reducing its contribution to traffic congestion. This might be another philosophy of urban taxi fleet management.

vii. The ideas and the strategies proposed here could be adapted to model car rental service as well as other demand responsive transportation modes, such as the paratransit operation in many countries.

viii. Lastly, there were several API modules (or plug-ins) created during the applications of the simulation model for this study, which could be readily used in future applications of PARAMICS. A few plug-ins to mention here are dynamic routing control plug-in (to control an individual vehicles routing behavior during simulation), and a plug-in to search for the link-to-link shortest path.

6.3 RECOMMENDATIONS FOR FUTURE RESEARCH

To further enhance the performance of the proposed system and utilize the system to its full potential, some directions for future research are proposed.

i. Future research may be continued to develop a comprehensive simulation model, which can simulate a mixture of both booking and street hailing behaviors. It would be more interesting if the booking problem can be addressed in conjunction with the service to roadside passengers, so as to precisely calculate the savings of empty cursing time and distances along the whole study horizon. In this research, street hailing is not simulated because of no real-life data available.

ⅱ. In addition, for the reason of commercial sensitivity, customer privacy and related issues, real-world demand sets of advance bookings are not easy to be accessed. As indicated in this study, the randomly generated data should be reasonably close to the real-world demand in the future when a large proportion of taxi demand is shifted from current booking and street hailing due to the low price to promote advance booking. As a matter of fact, this potential is verified by the survey results presented in Chapter 5. However, to further validate the merit of the proposed trip-chaining strategy, a test of a few of real world demand sets rather than randomly generated data sets is still remained as one of the future research tasks.

ⅲ. Finally, the study would be more complete if the dispatch strategy can chain the trips from both current bookings and advance bookings. In this study, the current bookings and advance booking were treated separately. However, it would be more efficient if the job package offered to a taxi driver consists of one current booking followed by several advance bookings. The idea is to minimize the negative effects of those advance bookings, which are just around half an hour later. As mentioned in Chapter 5, during this period of half an hour, if a driver tries to pick up roadside passengers, then the booking job may not be fulfilled on time. Conversely, if the driver gives up all the street pickup business, then it is apparently a waste of time and vehicle resource. Therefore, it would be better to link such a 'near' advance-booking request with a current booking job, where the drop off location and time of the current booking is reasonably close to the following advance booking request. In fact, with an overwhelmingly high number of current bookings against the advance bookings at present, it is possible to have this kind of match done successfully.

REFERENCES

[1] Abe, M. A. and B. C. Brush. On the regulation of price and service quality: The taxicab problem. *Quarterly Review of Economics and Business* ,1976,16: 105-111.

[2] Ahuja, R. K., K. Mehlhorn, J. B. Orlin and R. E. Tarjan. Faster algorithms for the shortest path problem. *Journal of ACM* ,1990,37:213-223.

[3] Alfa, A. S., S. S. Heragu, and M. Chen. A 3-opt based simulated annealing algorithm for vehicle routing problems. *Computers & Industrial Engineering* , 1991,21:635-639.

[4] Arnott, R. Taxi travel should be subsidized. *Journal of Urban Economics* , 1996,40:316-333.

[5] Barceló, J., Ferrer, J. L., García, D. and Grau, R. Microscopic traffic simulation for ATT systems analysis-A parallel computing version, *Contribution to the 25th Aniversary of CRT* . University of Montreal, 1998.

[6] Beesley, M. E. Regulation of taxis. *Economic Journal* ,1973,83:150-169.

[7] Beesley, M. E. and S. Glaister. Information for regulation: The case of taxis. *The Economic Journal* ,1983,93:594-615.

[8] Bellman, R. On a routing problem. *Quarter application mathematics* ,1958, 16:87-90.

[9] Bertsekas, D. P. An auction algorithm for shortest paths. SIAM, *journal on optimization* ,1991,1:435-447.

[10] Bertsekas, D. P. A simple and fast label-correcting algorithm for shortest paths. *Networks* ,1993,23:703-709.

[11] Bertsekas, D. P., F. Guerriero, and R. Musmanno. Parallel asynchronous label correcting methods for shortest paths. *Journal of Optimal Theory and Applications* ,1996,297-320.

[12] Bertsekas, D. P. *Network optimization: continuous and discrete models.* Athena Scientific, Belmont, Massachusetts, 1998.

[13] Bodin, L. D., B. L. Golden, A. A. Assad, and M. Ball. Routing and

scheduling of vehicles and crews, the state of the art. *Computers and Operations Research* ,1983,10(2): 63-212.

[14] Boxill, S. A. and Yu, L. An Evaluation of Traffic Simulation Models for Supporting ITS Development. Center for Transportation Training and Research, Texas Southern University, 2000.

[15] Cairns, R. D. and C. Liston-Heyes. Competition and regulation in the taxi industry. *Journal of Public Economics* ,1996,59:1-15.

[16] Carter, M. and D. Williamson. Quantitative Modeling For Management Business. New York: PITMAN Publishing,1996.

[17] Charles H. B. and H. C. Gerald. Survey Research, 2nd Edition. America: John Wiley& Sons Ltd. 1981:66-163.

[18] Chen, Z. L, W. B. Powell. A note on Bertsekas' small-label-first strategy. *Networks* ,1997,29:111-116.

[19] Cheng, Y. Singapore's Satellite-Based Taxi Tracking and Booking System, *ITE Journal website* : http://www. ite. org, Accessed Dec16, 2000.

[20] Christofides, N. Vehicle routing. In Lawler, E. L. , J. K. Lenstra, A. H. G. Rinnooy Kan, and D. B. Shmoys, editors, The Traveling Salesman Problem, Wiley, Chichester, UK,1985:431-448.

[21] Christofides, N. , A. Mingozzi, and P. Toth. The vehicle routing problem. In Christofides, N. , A. Mingozzi, P. Toth, and C. Sandi, editors, Combinatorial Optimization, Wiley, Chichester, UK, 1979:315-338.

[22] CityCab Pte Ltd website: http://www. citycab. com. sg Accessed Feb. 10, 2002.

[23] Clarke, G. and J . V. Wright. Scheduling of vehicles from a central depot to a number of delivery points. *Operations Research* ,1964,12:568-581.

[24] Clarke, G. and I. V. Wright. Scheduling of vehicles from a central depot to a number of delivery points. *Operations Research* ,1964,12:568-581.

[25] Comfort Transportation Pte Ltd. Website: http://www. comfort-transportation. com. sg Accessed Feb. 8 2002.

[26] Dantzig, G. B. and J. H. Ramser. The Truck Dispatching Problem. *Management Science* ,1959,6:80.

[27] David R. K. Methods of educational & social science research, an integrated approach, 2nd Edition. America: Addison-Wesley Educational Publishers,

Inc. 1998.

[28] Dempsey, P. S. Taxi industry regulation, deregulation and reregulation: The paradox of market failure. *Transportation Law Journal* ,1996,24:73-120.

[29] De vany, A. S. Capacity utilization under alternative regulatory constraints: An analysis of taxi markets. *Journal of Political Economy* ,1975,83:83-94.

[30] Desrochers, M. , J. K. Lenstra, and M. W. P. Savelsbergh. A classification scheme for vehicle routing and scheduling problems. *Journal of Operational Research Society* ,1990,46:322-332.

[31] Dial, R. B. , F. Glover, D. Karney and D. Klingman. A computational analysis of alternative algorithms and labeling techniques for finding shortest path trees. *Networks* ,1979,9:215-248.

[32] Dijkstra. E. W. A note on two problems in connection with graphs. *Numeriche Mathematik* ,1959,1:269-271.

[33] Douglas, G. W. Price regulation and optimal service standards: The taxicab industry. *Journal of Transport Economics and Policy* ,1972,20:116-127.

[34] Dror, M. editor. Arc Routing: Theory, Solutions and Applications. Kluwer, Boston, MA, 2000.

[35] Dumas, Y. , J. Desrosiers and F. Soumis. A dynamic programming solution of the large-scale single vehicle dial-a-ride problem with time windows, *American Journal of Mathematical and Management Science* ,1986,16:301-325.

[36] Dumas, Y. , J. Desrosiers and F. Soumis. The pick-up and delivery problem with time windows, *European Journal of Operational Research* ,1991,54:7-22.

[37] Federal Highway Administration. TSIS website: http://www.fhwa-tsis.com/ Accessed Feb. 10, 2002.

[38] Fisher, M. L. Vehicle routing. In Ball, M. O. , T. L. Magnanti, C. L. Monma, and G. L. Nemhauser, editors, Network Routing, Handbooks in Operations Research and Management Science 8, North-Holland, Amsterdam, 1995:1-33.

[39] Floyd, R. W. Algorithm 97, shortest path. *Communication ACM* , 5:345, 1962.

[40] Ford. L. R. and D. R. Fulkerson. Flows in networks. Princeton University

Press, Princeton, NJ, 1987.

[41] Foerster, J. F. and G. Gilbert. Taxicab deregulation: Economic consequences and regulatory choices. *Transportation*, 1979, 8: 371-387.

[42] Frankena, M. W. and P. A. Pautier. Taxicab regulation: An economic analysis. *Research in Law and Economics*, 1986, 9: 129-165.

[43] Friedman, M. Price theory: A provisional text. Aldine, Chicago: Aldine Publishing Co. 1962.

[44] Fredman, M. L. and R. E. Tarjan. Fibonacci heaps and their uses in improved network optimization algorithms, 1987.

[45] Gallick, E. C. and D. E. Sisk. A reconsideration of taxi regulation. *Journal of Law, Economics and Organization*, 1987, 3(1): 117-128.

[46] Gaunt, C. Information for regulators: the case of taxicab license prices. *International Journal of Transport Economics*, 1996, XXIII(3): 331-345.

[47] Gaunt, C. and Black, T. The economic cost of taxicab regulation: The case of Brisbane. *Economic Analysis and Policy*, 1996, 26(1): 45-58.

[48] Garling, T., T. Laitila, A. Marell and K. Westin. A note on the short-term effects of deregulation of the Swedish taxicab industry. *Journal of Transport Economics and Policy*, 1995, 29(2): 209-214.

[49] Gallo, G. and S. Pallottino. Shortest path methods in transportation models. In (M. Florian, ed.) Transportation planning models, North-Holland, 1984: 227-256.

[50] Gallo, G. and S. Pallottino. Shortest path algorithms. *Annals of operation research*, 1988, 7: 3-79.

[51] Gendreau, M., A. Hertz, and G. Laporte. A tabu search heuristic for the vehicle routing problem. *Management Science*, 1994, 40: 1276-1290.

[52] Gillett, B. E. and L. R. Miller. A heuristic algorithm for the vehicle dispatch problem. *Operations Research*, 1974, 22: 340-349.

[53] Glover, F., D. Klingman and N. Philips. A new polynomially bounded shortest path algorithm. *Operation Research*, 1985, 33: 65-73.

[54] Glover, F. and M. Laguna. Tabu Search. Kluwer, Boston, MA, 1997.

[55] Golden, B. L. and A. A. Assad. Vehicle Routing: Methods and Studies. North- Holland, Amsterdam, 1988.

[56] Golden, B. L., E. A. Wasil, J. P. Kelly, and I. M. Chao. Metaheuristics in

vehicle routing. In T. G Crainic and G. Laporte, editors, Fleet Management and Logistics, Kluwer, Boston, MA,1998:33-56.

[57] Goldberg, A. V. and T. Radzik. A heuristic improvement of the Bellman-Ford algorithm. Application mathematics letter,1993,6:3-6.

[58] Golob, T. F and A. C. Regan. Impacts of Highway Congestion on Freight Operations: Perceptions of Trucking Industry Managers. Working paper, University of California, Irvine, 1999.

[59] Hackner, J. and S. Nyberg. Deregulating taxi services: A word of caution. *Journal of Transport Economics and Policy* ,1995,29:195-207.

[60] Holland, J. H. Adaptation in Natural and Artificial Systems. The University of Michigan Press, Ann Arbor, MI, 1975.

[61] Innovative Transportation Concepts, Inc.'s VISSIM website: http://www.itc—world.com/ Accessed Feb. 12, 2002.

[62] Kaufman, D. E. and R. L. Smith. Fastest paths in time-dependent networks for intelligent vehicle-highway systems applications. *IVHS Journal* ,1993,1:1-11.

[63] Kayne, J. and T. Rubel. A Governor's Guide to Intelligent Transportation System/Commercial Vehicle Operations. National Governors Association, 1997.

[64] Land Transport Authority. White Paper: A World Class Land Transport System, 1996:8.

[65] Laporte, G. The vehicle routing problem: An overview of exact and approximate algorithms. *European Journal of Operational Research* , 1992, 59:345-358.

[66] Laporte, G. and Y. Nobert. Exact algorithms for the vehicle routing problem. *Annals of Discrete Mathematics* ,1987,31:147-184.

[67] Laporte, G. Vehicle routing. In Arnico, M. D., F. Maffioli, and S. Martello, editors, Annotated Bibliographies in Combinatorial Optimization, Wiley, Chichester, UK, 1997.

[68] Laporte, G. and I. H. Osman. Routing problems: A bibliography. *Annals of Operations Research* ,1995,61:227-262.

[69] Lau, H. C. and Z., Liang. Pickup and delivery problem with time windows: algorithms and test case generation, *International Journal of Artificial*

Intelligence Tools ,2002,11(3):455-472.

[70] Lawler, E. L. , I. K. Lenstra, A. H. G. Rinnooy Kan, and D. B. Shmoys, The Traveling Salesman Problem. Wiley, Chichester, UK, 1985.

[71] Lee, J. GPS Taxi Dispatching System. *Proceedings of the 1st Asia Pacific Conference on Transportation and the Environment* , Singapore, May 13-15, 1998.

[72] Li, H. and A. Lim. A metaheuristic for the pickup and delivery problem with time windows, *13th IEEE International Conference on Tools with Artificial Intelligence* (ICTAI'01), Dallas, Texas, U. S. , Nov 7-9, 2001.

[73] Lin, S. Computer solutions of the traveling salesman problem. *Bell System Technical Journal* ,1965,44:2245-2269.

[74] Lipsey, R. G. and P. Steiner. *Economics* , Harper-Row, New York. 1966.

[75] Magnanti, T. L. Combinatorial optimization and vehicle fleet planning: Perspectives and prospects. *Networks* ,1981,11:179-214.

[76] Manski, C. F. and J. D. Wright. Nature of equilibrium in the market for taxi services. *Transportation Research Record* ,1976,619:296-306.

[77] Martello, S. and P. Toth. Knapsack Problems: Algorithms and Computer Implementations, Wiley, Chichester, UK, 1990.

[78] Ministry of Law. Singapore Street Directory, 20th edition, SNP Publishing, Singapore, pp. 610, 2000.

[79] Moor, E. F. The shortest path through a maze. In *Proceedings of the International Symposium on Theory of Switching* , 285-292. Harvard University Press, 1957.

[80] Morrison, P. S. Restructuring effects of deregulation: The case of the New Zealand taxi industry. *Environment and Planning* , 1997,29A:913-928.

[81] Orr, D. The taxicab problem: A proposed solution. *Journal of Political Economy* ,1969,77:141-147.

[82] Osman, I. H. Meta-strategy simulated annealing and tabu search algorithms for the vehicle routing problem. *Annals of Operations Research* ,1993,41: 421-451.

[83] Pallottino, S. Adaptation de l´algorithme de d´esopo-pape pour la determination de tous les chemins les plus courts: ameliorations et simplifications. Technical Reports 136, Centre de recherche sur les

Transports, Universite de Montreal, 1979.

[84] Pallottino, S. , M. Scutellà. Shortest Path Algorithms in Transportation Models: Classical and Innovative Aspects. *Technical Report: TR-97-06*, *University of Pisa* , 1997.

[85] Palma, D. , P. Hansen and M. Labbe. Commuters' paths with penalties for early or late arrival times. *Transportation Science* ,1993,24:276-286.

[86] Pape, U. Implementation and efficiency of moore-algorithms for the shortest path problem. *Mathematical Programming* ,1974,7:212-222.

[87] Psarafis, H. A dynamic programming solution to the single vehicle many-to-many immediate request dial-a-ride problem, *Transportation Science* ,1980, 14:130-154.

[88] Psarafis, H. An exact algorithm for the single vehicle many-to-many immediate request dial-a-ride problem, *Transportation Science* ,1983,17(4): 351-361.

[89] Quadstone Limited. PARAMICS Modeler V3. 0 User Guide and Reference Manual. Quadstone Ltd, Edinburgh, United Kingdom, 2000.

[90] Radbone, I. Looking at Adelaide's taxi industry. *Road and Transport Research* ,1998,7(2):52-59.

[91] Regan, A. C. and T. F. Golob. Freight Operations' Perceptions of Congestion Problems and the Application of Advanced Technologies: Results from a 1998 Survey of 1200 Companies Operating in California. Working paper, University of California, Irvine, 1999.

[92] Robuste, F. , C. F. Daganzo, and R. Souleyrette. Implementing vehicle routing models. *Transportation Research B* ,1990,24:263-286.

[93] Rochat, Y. and E. D. Taillard. Probabilistic diversification and intensification in local search for vehicle routing. *Journal of Heuristics* ,1995,1:147-167.

[94] Rornetsch, S. and E. Wolfstetter. The taxicab market: An elementary model. *Journal of Institutional and Theoretical Economics* ,1993,149(3):531-546.

[95] Ryan, D. M. , C. Hjorring, and F. Glover. Extensions of the petal method for vehicle routing. *Journal of Operational Research Society* ,1993,44:289-296.

[96] Salant, P. and D. A. Dillman. How to Conduct Your Own Survey. New

York: Wiley. 1994.

[97] Savelsbergh, M. W. P. Local search for routing problems with time windows. *Annals of Operations Research* ,1995,4:285-305.

[98] Saw S. H. A guide to conducting surveys, 38-47, Singapore: Times Editions Pte Ltd. 1990.

[99] Schaller, B. Elasticities for taxicab fares and service availability. *Transportation* ,1999,26:283-297.

[100] Sexton, T. R. and D. B. Lawrence. Optimizing single vehicle many-to-many dial-a-ride problem with desired delivery time: I scheduling, *Transportation Science* ,1985,19:378-410.

[101] Sexton, T. R. and D. B. Lawrence. Optimizing single vehicle many-to-many dial-a-ride problem with desired delivery time: II routing, *Transportation Science* ,1985,19:411-435.

[102] Sexton, T. R. and Y. -Y. Choi. Pickup and delivery partial loads with "soft" time windows, *American Journal of Mathematical and Management Science* ,1986,6:369-398.

[103] Shrieber, C. The economic reasons for price and entry regulation of taxicabs. *Journal of Transport Economics and Policy* ,1975,9:268-293.

[104] Shrieber, C. A rejoinder. *Journal of Transport Economics and Policy* ,1977, 11:298-304.

[105] Solomon, M. M. Algorithms for the vehicle routing and scheduling problems with time window constrains, *Operations Research* ,1987,35:254-264.

[106] Taillard, E. D. Parallel iterative search methods for vehicle routing problems. *Networks* ,1993,23:661-673.

[107] Teal, R. F. and B. Berglund. The impacts of taxicab deregulation in the USA. *Journal of Transport Economics and Policy* ,1987,21:37-56.

[108] TIBS Taxis Pte Ltd website: http://www. tibs. com. sg Accessed Feb. 8, 2002.

[109] Toth, P. and D. Vigo. Exact algorithms for vehicle routing. In Crainic, T. and G. Laporte, editors, Fleet Management and Logistics, Kluwer, Boston, MA, 1998: 1-31.

[110] Transport Department, The level of taxi services. TTSD Publication Series, Hong Kong Government, Hong Kong . 1986-2000.

[111] Transport Simulation Systems (GETRAM) website: http://www.tss-bcn.com/ Accessed Feb. 12, 2002.

[112] Van Aerde, M. and the Transportation Research Group. INTEGRATION Release 2 User's Guide-Volume 1: Fundamental model features. Queen's University, Kingston, Ontario, Canada, 1999.

[113] Van der Bruggen, L. J. J., J. K. Lenstra and P. C. Schuur. Variable-depth search for the single vehicle pickup and delivery problem with time windows, *Transportation Science*, 1993, 27: 298-311.

[114] Van Vliet, D. Improved shortest path algorithms for transport networks. *Transportation research*, 1978, 12: 7-20.

[115] Warshall, S. A theorem on Boolean matrices. *Journal ACM*, 1962, 9: 11-12.

[116] William, P. N. and J. W. Barnes, Solving the pickup and delivery problem with time windows using tabu search, *Transportation Research*, Part B, 2000, 34: 107-121.

[117] Williams, J. W. J. Algorithm 232: heapsort. Communications of the ACM. 1964, 7: 347-348.

[118] Wren, A. and A. Holliday. Computer scheduling of vehicles from one or more depots to a number of delivery points. *Operational Research*, 1972, 23: 333-344.

[119] Wren, A. Computers in Transport Planning and Operation. Ian Allan, London, 1971.

[120] Wong, K. I., S. C. Wong and H. Yang. Modeling urban taxi services in congested road networks with elastic demand. *Transportation Research*, 2001, 35B: 819-842.

[121] Xu, J. M., S. C. Wong, H. Yang and C. 0. Tong. Modeling the level of urban taxi services using a neural network *Journal of Transportation Engineering*, ASCE, 1999, 125(3): 216-223.

[122] Xu, J. and J. P. Kelly. A network flow-based tabu search heuristic for the vehicle routing problem. *Transportation Science*, 1996, 30: 379-393.

[123] Yellow-Top Cab Pte Ltd. website: http://www.yellow-top-cab.com.sg Accessed Feb. 8, 2002.

[124] Yang, H., Y. W. Lau, S. C. Wong and H. K. Lo. A macroscopic taxi model for passenger demand, taxi utilization and level of services.

Transportation , 1998,27:317-340.

[125] Yang, H. and S. C. Wong. Modeling urban taxi services: A network equilibrium approach. *Proceedings of the Second Conference of Hong Kong Society for Transportation Studies* , Hong Kong, 6 December 1997,1997:15-20.

[126] Yang, H. and S. C. Wong. A network model of urban taxi services. *Transportation Research* ,1998,32B:235-246.

[127] Yang, H. , S. C. Wong and K. 1. Wong. Modeling urban taxi services in road networks: Progress, problem and prospect. *Journal of Advanced Transportation* ,2001,35:237-258.

[128] Yang, H. , S. C. Wong and K. 1. Wong. Demand-supply equilibrium of taxi services in a network under competition and regulation. *Transportation Research* ,2002,36B:799-819.

[129] Wong, K. I. , S. C. Wong, H. Yang and C. O. Tong. A sensitivity-based solution algorithm for the network model of urban taxi services. *Proceedings of the 15th International Symposium on Transportation and Traffic Theory* , Pergamon. 2002.

Appendix A: Sample Output File for Simulation Run

```
======================================================
demand_location     link_name     demand_time    Simulation_begin     Warmup_time
      145              52:51          61800            61200               600
======================================================
the total number of taxi is : 100
Actually, the taxi searched by New method is: top   20 (based on xy_dist)
======================================================
  the link_id on which each taxi is located when demand is confirmed
======================================================
 i_taxi       taxi_id(long)         link_id   link_name
    1            80683736            1054     358:541
    2          1113063424            1261     431:648
    3            80683848             733     248:299
    4            80683904             852     288:399
    5            80683960            1029     350:437
    6            80684016             578     194:195
    7            80684072              94      37:786
    8            80684128             395     136:459
    9            80684184             115      43:147
   10            80684240             862     292:291
   11            80684296            1398     495:191
   12          1115422720             286     101:619
   13            80684408             343     120:709
   14            80684464            1915     758:166
   15          1110966272            1613     604:605
   16            80684576            1030     350:292
   17          1119748096              80      31:463
   18          1113587712            2180     898:328
   19            80684744            1970     787:24
   20            80684800             404     139:769
   21          1119879168              94      37:786
```

```
 22       80684912      958     325:394
 23     1118437376      679     230:771
 24     1119223808      540     182:815
              .
              .
              .
              .
 88       80688552      870     294:404
 89       80688608     2012     809:865
 90       80688664      121      45:42
 91       80688720      205      75:121
 92       80688776      339     119:657
 93       80688832      119      44:55
 94       80688888     1763     675:372
 95       80688944      597     202:499
 96       80689000      515     175:731
 97       80689056     1683     635:248
 98       80689112     1795     693:694
 99       80689168     1036     352:629
100       80689224      141      51:69
===============================================
============== New method (when demand is confirmed) ==============
The ETA is 17.000000 and the suit_taxi is 4    taxi_id is 80683904
===============================================
704:11 turn 2    109:106 turn 1    106:708 turn 2    708:52 turn 1
52:51,travel dist:309.4

when demand come: suit_taxi was at        207:704(link 612)
direct dist to demand location is 406.14

============== XY method    (when demand is confirmed) ==============
xy_ETA is 58.000000 and the xy_suit_taxi is 36    taxi_id is 80685696
===============================================
 69:12 turn 2     120:709 turn 1     709:119 turn 1     119:657 turn 1
657:54 turn 1      54:503 turn 1     503:118 turn 1     118:46 turn 1
 46:41 turn 2      41:109 turn 1     109:106 turn 1     106:708 turn 2
708:52 turn 1        52:51,travel dist:1165.6
when demand come: xy_suit_taxi was at        51:69(link 141)
```

```
direct dist to demand location is 34.47

====================total travel distance ====================

total travel distance for new method is 356.43
total travel distance for xy method is 1262.56

==========================================================



==========================================================
  Simulation begin at 61200
==========================================================
Demand time: 61800, demand location: 52:51 (link    145)

 (new) taxi arrive at time =  61811.000000
 ( xy) taxi arrive at time =  61943.500000

    new_time =  11.000000
     xy_time =  143.500000
improve_time =  132.500000
```

Appendix B: Simulation Results for Empty Taxi Rate 5%

Table B. 1 Simulation Results for Parco Bugis

Run No.	Taxi Identified	Travel Distance/m		Improvement in Distance/m	Travel Time/s		Improvement in Time/s
		Current System	Proposed System		Current System	Proposed System	
1	Different	1263	1223	39	144	11	133
2	Different	1263	164	1099	139	34	105
3	Same	—	—	0	149	149	0
4	Different	1263	164	1099	303	66	237
5	Different	1263	1216	46	157	57	100
6	Different	1174	164	1010	290	67	223
7	Different	1263	164	1099	132	86	46
8	Different	1263	110	1153	242	34	208
9	Different	1228	356	872	292	13	279
10	Different	1461	929	531	152	68	84
Average		1271	499	695	200	58	141

Table B. 2 Simulation Results for Golden Mile

Run No.	Taxi Identified	Travel Distance/m		Improvement in Distance/m	Travel Time/s		Improvement in Time/s
		Current System	Proposed System		Current System	Proposed System	
1	Different	1638	1572	65	148	72	76
2	Same	—	—	0	223	223	0
3	Different	4852	2023	2828	399	282	117
4	Different	1645	367	1277	168	72	96
5	Different	2989	2023	965	427	158	269
6	Same	—	—	0	135	135	0
7	Same	—	—	0	128	128	0
8	Same	—	—	0	262	262	0
9	Different	2158	1963	194	328	231	97
10	Same	—	—	0	61	61	0
Average		2656	1590	533	228	162	65

Table B. 3 Simulation Results for Raffles Place

Run No.	Taxi Identified	Travel Distance/m		Improvement in Distance/m	Travel Time/s		Improvement in Time/s
		Current System	Proposed System		Current System	Proposed System	
1	Different	1787	730	1056	189	42	147
2	Different	1712	760	952	250	110	140
3	Different	1789	1222	567	310	201	109
4	Different	1798	1156	641	261	81	180
5	Different	1438	309	1129	168	69	99
6	Different	1695	480	1215	131	64	67
7	Different	1506	290	1216	190	44	146
8	Different	1695	364	1331	250	141	110
9	Different	1695	309	1386	201	111	90
10	Same	—	—	0	9	9	0
Average		1679	625	949	196	87	109

Table B. 4 Simulation Results for Suntec City

Run No.	Taxi Identified	Travel Distance/m		Improvement in Distance/m	Travel Time/s		Improvement in Time/s
		Current System	Proposed System		Current System	Proposed System	
1	Same	—	—	0	123	123	0
2	Different	2774	1213	1562	270	183	87
3	Different	2252	1190	1062	331	149	182
4	Different	2007	1691	316	209	133	76
5	Same	—	—	0	112	112	0
6	Same	—	—	0	61	61	0
7	Different	1412	590	822	209	69	140
8	Different	745	502	243	50	32	18
9	Same	—	—	0	244	244	0
10	Different	1968	1068	900	160	119	41
Average		1860	1042	490	177	122	54

Table B. 5 Simulation Results for Mt. Elizabeth

Run No.	Taxi Identified	Travel Distance/m		Improvement in Distance/m	Travel Time/s		Improvement in Time/s
		Current System	Proposed System		Current System	Proposed System	
1	Different	1056	416	641	153	133	20
2	Different	1250	736	514	184	22	163
3	Different	1114	186	929	250	10	240
4	Same	—	—	0	73	73	0
5	Same	—	—	0	5	5	0
6	Different	998	416	583	117	21	97
7	Same	—	—	0	189	189	0
8	Same	—	—	0	20	20	0
9	Different	876	736	140	124	23	102
10	Different	1056	484	572	114	60	54
Average		1059	496	338	123	55	67

Table B. 6 Simulation Results for Shenton Way

Run No.	Taxi Identified	Travel Distance/m		Improvement in Distance/m	Travel Time/s		Improvement in Time/s
		Current System	Proposed System		Current System	Proposed System	
1	Different	2135	1012	1123	230	48	182
2	Different	2256	884	1373	177	48	129
3	Different	2234	1106	1128	236	106	130
4	Different	2163	960	1203	168	50	119
5	Different	2135	1106	1029	288	110	178
6	Different	2290	1012	1277	243	49	194
7	Different	2135	695	1440	228	50	178
8	Different	2290	1012	1277	288	51	238
9	Different	2246	923	1323	185	58	127
10	Different	2338	1359	979	115	65	50
Average		2222	1007	1215	216	63	152

Table B.7 Simulation Results for Maxwell Road

Run No.	Taxi Identified	Travel Distance/m		Improvement in Distance/m	Travel Time/s		Improvement in Time/s
		Current System	Proposed System		Current System	Proposed System	
1	Different	2112	649	1463	244	21	223
2	Different	2062	240	1821	123	13	111
3	Different	2112	1178	934	274	85	189
4	Same	—	—	0	246	246	0
5	Same	—	—	0	14	14	0
6	Different	1905	816	1089	184	73	111
7	Different	1019	0	1019	44	5	39
8	Different	1996	1121	875	161	74	87
9	Different	1019	0	1019	49	1	49
10	Different	1732	980	752	212	95	117
Average		1745	623	897	155	62	92

Table B.8 Simulation Results for Chinatown

Run No.	Taxi Identified	Travel Distance/m		Improvement in Distance/m	Travel Time/s		Improvement in Time/s
		Current System	Proposed System		Current System	Proposed System	
1	Different	1168	734	434	135	15	120
2	Different	1669	1421	248	172	51	121
3	Same	—	—	0	169	169	0
4	Same	—	—	0	111	111	0
5	Different	2148	720	1428	234	42	192
6	Same	—	—	0	1	1	0
7	Different	1691	734	958	214	51	163
8	Different	1083	1037	46	124	91	33
9	Different	820	734	87	36	43	−7
10	Different	1298	252	1045	72	44	28
Average		1411	805	425	126	62	65

Table B. 9 Simulation Results for Orchard Rd

Run No.	Taxi Identified	Travel Distance/m		Improvement in Distance/m	Travel Time/s		Improvement in Time/s
		Current System	Proposed System		Current System	Proposed System	
1	Different	1328	509	820	220	17	203
2	Different	1451	436	1015	302	54	249
3	Same	—	—	0	3	3	0
4	Different	2335	175	2160	317	1	316
5	Different	1328	823	505	199	92	107
6	Same	—	—	0	1	1	0
7	Different	1333	263	1070	158	11	147
8	Different	1451	175	1276	168	3	165
9	Different	1333	745	588	130	79	51
10	Different	1333	436	897	114	59	55
Average		1487	445	833	161	32	129

Table B. 10 Simulation Results for Selegie Rd

Run No.	Taxi Identified	Travel Distance/m		Improvement in Distance/m	Travel Time/s		Improvement in Time/s
		Current System	Proposed System		Current System	Proposed System	
1	Different	1638	260	1378	104	13	91
2	Same	—	—	0	74	74	0
3	Different	872	225	647	46	67	−21
4	Same	—	—	0	88	88	0
5	Different	798	904	−106	66	151	−85
6	Different	1196	683	512	212	68	144
7	Same	—	—	0	93	93	0
8	Same	—	—	0	77	77	0
9	Same	—	—	0	46	46	0
10	Different	1109	893	217	166	50	116
Average		1123	593	265	97	73	25

Appendix C: Time Improvement Matrices for Various Empty Rates

Table C. 1 Improvements in Time for 5% Empty Taxi Rate

Run No.	Location									
	Parco Bugis	Golden Mile	Boat Quay	Suntec City	Mt. Elizabeth	Shenton Way	Maxwell Rd	China-town	Orchard Rd	Selegie Rd
1	132.5	76	147	0	20	181.5	223	120.5	203	91
2	104.5	0	139.5	87	162.5	128.5	110.5	121	248.5	0
3	0	117	109	182	240	130	188.5	0	0	−21
4	236.5	96	180	76	0	118.5	0	0	316	0
5	99.5	268.5	99	0	0	178	0	192	107	−85
6	223	0	67	0	96.5	194	111	0	0	144
7	46	0	145.5	140	0	178	39	163	146.5	0
8	208	0	109.5	18	0	237.5	87	32.5	165	0
9	279	97	90	0	101.5	127	48.5	−7	50.5	0
10	83.5	0	0	41	54	50	117	27.5	54.5	116

Table C. 2 Improvements in Time for 10% Empty Taxi Rate

Run No.	Location									
	Parco Bugis	Golden Mile	Boat Quay	Suntec City	Mt. Elizabeth	Shenton Way	Maxwell Rd	China-town	Orchard Rd	Selegie Rd
1	39.5	88.5	0	177.5	124	115.5	0	315.5	102	45.5
2	93.5	203	0	0	109	124.5	−12.5	77.5	135.5	177
3	55	104	136.5	39.5	0	180.5	0	155.5	0	153
4	0	91.5	31	19	0	193.5	68.5	0	0	0
5	108	43	0	0	134.5	243	208	105	238	0
6	142.5	78	208.5	0	192.5	60	0	257.5	149	0
7	10.5	201.5	0	−5.5	58.5	110	165	148.5	144	88.5
8	206.5	0	198.5	0	168.5	79	2.5	0	144	231
9	216	116	147.5	190.5	0	122.5	227	0	327.5	0
10	116	0	0	0	162	10.5	8	0	192	99.5

Table C. 3 Improvements in Time for 15% Empty Taxi Rate

Run No.	Location									
	Parco Bugis	Golden Mile	Boat Quay	Suntec City	Mt. Elizabeth	Shenton Way	Maxwell Rd	China-town	Orchard Rd	Selegie Rd
1	36.5	190	103.5	11.5	150	79	0	0	122	83.5
2	177.5	76.5	246	169	164	179.5	0	141	0	58
3	55	0	88.5	278.5	194	67	119.5	−96.5	0	73
4	139.5	0	40.5	0	145	134.5	0	118	0	19
5	73.5	64	82	0	151.5	178	0	0	0	0
6	0	0	172.5	0	0	220	0	−22	118.5	0
7	126.5	179	−34.5	21.5	163	177.5	149	176.5	141.5	0
8	94	0	246.5	0	178.5	238.5	194	91	0	169
9	232.5	376	90	66	0	−69.5	37.5	159.5	89.5	98
10	99.5	84	243	0	81.5	79	56.5	55	246	0

Appendix D: Randomly Generated Demand Sets

Table D.1 One Set of Randomly Generated Demand with Time Deviations of 15.1 min

Booking Request	Pickup Location	Destination Location	Pickup Time
1	The Paragon Tower	Parco Bugis Junction	8:30PM
2	Cairnhill Place	Bank of China	8:45PM
3	Sunshine Plaza	People's Park Complex	8:50PM
4	Sin Tai Hin Building	Centennial Tower	8:35PM
5	Parco Bugis Junction	Maxwell Road Food Center	8:25PM
6	Bugis Village	UIC Building	8:25PM
7	Golden Mile Complex	Air View Building	8:15PM
8	Keypoint Building	People's Park Complex	8:45PM
9	Ngee Ann City	OUB Center	8:25PM
10	Singapore Power Building	Centennial Tower	8:55PM
11	Suntec City Tower	Sunshine Plaza	8:50PM
12	Centennial Tower	Air View Building	7:50PM
13	People's Park Complex	Ngee Ann City	8: 5PM
14	Ministry of Manpower	Golden Mile Complex	8:10PM
15	OUB Center	The Paragon Tower	8:25PM
16	Bank of China	Golden Mile Complex	8:10PM
17	Maxwell Road Food Center	CPF Building	8: 5PM
18	Air View Building	Sin Tai Hin Building	8:35PM
19	CPF Building	Ngee Ann City	8:40PM
20	UIC Building	Bugis Village	8:50PM
21	Cairnhill Place	People's Park Complex	8:15PM
22	The Paragon Tower	Centennial Tower	8:50PM
23	Sunshine Plaza	Air View Building	9: 0PM
24	Sin Tai Hin Building	CPF Building	8: 5PM
25	Parco Bugis Junction	Cairnhill Place	8:30PM
26	Bugis Village	People's Park Complex	8: 5PM
27	Golden Mile Complex	Parco Bugis Junction	7:55PM

Table D. 1 (Continued)

Booking Request	Pickup Location	Destination Location	Pickup Time
28	Keypoint Building	Bank of China	8:15PM
29	Singapore Power Building	Sunshine Plaza	8:30PM
30	Ngee Ann City	Air View Building	8:35PM
31	Centennial Tower	Ngee Ann City	8:35PM
32	Suntec City Tower	Golden Mile Complex	8:45PM
33	Ministry of Manpower	OUB Center	8:35PM
34	People's Park Complex	Centennial Tower	8:15PM
35	Bank of China	CPF Building	8: 5PM
36	OUB Center	Sin Tai Hin Building	8:20PM
37	Air View Building	Ngee Ann City	8:10PM
38	Maxwell Road Food Center	Bugis Village	8:15PM
39	UIC Building	The Paragon Tower	8:10PM
40	CPF Building	Golden Mile Complex	8:40PM
Average Deviation of Pickup Time: $\sum_{i=1}^{n} \mid T_i - \overline{T} \mid / n$			15.1 (min)

Table D. 2　One Set of Randomly Generated Demand with Time Deviations of 23.6 min

Booking Request	Pickup Location	Destination Location	Pickup Time
1	The Paragon Tower	Parco Bugis Junction	8:30PM
2	Cairnhill Place	Bank of China	9:15PM
3	Sunshine Plaza	People's Park Complex	8:55PM
4	Sin Tai Hin Building	Centennial Tower	8:35PM
5	Parco Bugis Junction	Maxwell Road Food Center	8:25PM
6	Bugis Village	UIC Building	8:25PM
7	Golden Mile Complex	Air View Building	8:15PM
8	Keypoint Building	People's Park Complex	8:45PM
9	Ngee Ann City	OUB Center	8:25PM
10	Singapore Power Building	Centennial Tower	9:25PM
11	Suntec City Tower	Sunshine Plaza	8:50PM
12	Centennial Tower	Air View Building	7:45PM
13	People's Park Complex	Ngee Ann City	8: 5PM
14	Ministry of Manpower	Golden Mile Complex	8:10PM
15	OUB Center	The Paragon Tower	8:25PM
16	Bank of China	Golden Mile Complex	8:10PM

Table D. 2(Continued)

Booking Request	Pickup Location	Destination Location	Pickup Time
17	Maxwell Road Food Center	CPF Building	8:05PM
18	Air View Building	Sin Tai Hin Building	8:40PM
19	CPF Building	Ngee Ann City	9:20PM
20	UIC Building	Bugis Village	8:50PM
21	Cairnhill Place	People's Park Complex	7:45PM
22	The Paragon Tower	Centennial Tower	8:50PM
23	Sunshine Plaza	Air View Building	9:10PM
24	Sin Tai Hin Building	CPF Building	8:05PM
25	Parco Bugis Junction	Cairnhill Place	9:40PM
26	Bugis Village	People's Park Complex	8: 0PM
27	Golden Mile Complex	Parco Bugis Junction	7:50PM
28	Keypoint Building	Bank of China	8:15PM
29	Singapore Power Building	Sunshine Plaza	9:05PM
30	Ngee Ann City	Air View Building	9:00PM
31	Centennial Tower	Ngee Ann City	8:35PM
32	Suntec City Tower	Golden Mile Complex	8:45PM
33	Ministry of Manpower	OUB Center	8:35PM
34	People's Park Complex	Centennial Tower	7:55PM
35	Bank of China	CPF Building	8:05PM
36	OUB Center	Sin Tai Hin Building	8:20PM
37	Air View Building	Ngee Ann City	8:10PM
38	Maxwell Road Food Center	Bugis Village	8:15PM
39	UIC Building	The Paragon Tower	7:50PM
40	CPF Building	Golden Mile Complex	8:40PM
Average Deviation of Pickup Time: $\sum_{i=1}^{n} \mid T_i - \overline{T} \mid / n$			23.6 (min)

Table D. 3 One Set of Randomly Generated Demand with Time Deviations of 30. 6 min

Booking Request	Pickup Location	Destination Location	Pickup Time
1	The Paragon Tower	Parco Bugis Junction	8:30PM
2	Cairnhill Place	Bank of China	9:15PM
3	Sunshine Plaza	People's Park Complex	8:55PM
4	Sin Tai Hin Building	Centennial Tower	8:35PM
5	Parco Bugis Junction	Maxwell Road Food Center	8:25PM

Table D. 3 (Continued)

Booking Request	Pickup Location	Destination Location	Pickup Time
6	Bugis Village	UIC Building	8:25PM
7	Golden Mile Complex	Air View Building	8:15PM
8	Keypoint Building	People's Park Complex	8:45PM
9	Ngee Ann City	OUB Center	8:25PM
10	Singapore Power Building	Centennial Tower	9:25PM
11	Suntec City Tower	Sunshine Plaza	8:50PM
12	Centennial Tower	Air View Building	7:45PM
13	People's Park Complex	Ngee Ann City	8:05PM
14	Ministry of Manpower	Golden Mile Complex	8:10PM
15	OUB Center	The Paragon Tower	9:45PM
16	Bank of China	Golden Mile Complex	8:10PM
17	Maxwell Road Food Center	CPF Building	8:05PM
18	Air View Building	Sin Tai Hin Building	8:40PM
19	CPF Building	Ngee Ann City	9:20PM
20	UIC Building	Bugis Village	8:50PM
21	Cairnhill Place	People's Park Complex	6:45PM
22	The Paragon Tower	Centennial Tower	8:50PM
23	Sunshine Plaza	Air View Building	9:10PM
24	Sin Tai Hin Building	CPF Building	8:05PM
25	Parco Bugis Junction	Cairnhill Place	9:40PM
26	Bugis Village	People's Park Complex	8:00PM
27	Golden Mile Complex	Parco Bugis Junction	7:15PM
28	Keypoint Building	Bank of China	8:15PM
29	Singapore Power Building	Sunshine Plaza	9:05PM
30	Ngee Ann City	Air View Building	9:00PM
31	Centennial Tower	Ngee Ann City	8:35PM
32	Suntec City Tower	Golden Mile Complex	8:45PM
33	Ministry of Manpower	OUB Center	9:55PM
34	People's Park Complex	Centennial Tower	7:55PM
35	Bank of China	CPF Building	7:35PM
36	OUB Center	Sin Tai Hin Building	8:20PM
37	Air View Building	Ngee Ann City	8:10PM
38	Maxwell Road Food Center	Bugis Village	8:15PM
39	UIC Building	The Paragon Tower	7:50PM
40	CPF Building	Golden Mile Complex	8:40PM
Average Deviation of Pickup Time: $\sum_{i=1}^{n} \mid T_i - \overline{T} \mid / n$			30.6 (min)

Table D. 4 One Set of Randomly Generated Demand with Time Deviations of 46. 4 min

Booking Request	Pickup Location	Destination Location	Pickup Time
1	The Paragon Tower	Parco Bugis Junction	9:30PM
2	Cairnhill Place	Bank of China	9:55PM
3	Sunshine Plaza	People's Park Complex	8:55PM
4	Sin Tai Hin Building	Centennial Tower	8:35PM
5	Parco Bugis Junction	Maxwell Road Food Center	8:25PM
6	Bugis Village	UIC Building	8:25PM
7	Golden Mile Complex	Air View Building	7:35PM
8	Keypoint Building	People's Park Complex	10:30PM
9	Ngee Ann City	OUB Center	8:25PM
10	Singapore Power Building	Centennial Tower	9:25PM
11	Suntec City Tower	Sunshine Plaza	8:50PM
12	Centennial Tower	Air View Building	7:45PM
13	People's Park Complex	Ngee Ann City	8:05PM
14	Ministry of Manpower	Golden Mile Complex	8:10PM
15	OUB Center	The Paragon Tower	9:45PM
16	Bank of China	Golden Mile Complex	8:10PM
17	Maxwell Road Food Center	CPF Building	8:05PM
18	Air View Building	Sin Tai Hin Building	9:30PM
19	CPF Building	Ngee Ann City	9:30PM
20	UIC Building	Bugis Village	8:50PM
21	Cairnhill Place	People's Park Complex	6:45PM
22	The Paragon Tower	Centennial Tower	8:50PM
23	Sunshine Plaza	Air View Building	9:10PM
24	Sin Tai Hin Building	CPF Building	8:00PM
25	Parco Bugis Junction	Cairnhill Place	9:40PM
26	Bugis Village	People's Park Complex	8:00PM
27	Golden Mile Complex	Parco Bugis Junction	6:30PM
28	Keypoint Building	Bank of China	8:15PM
29	Singapore Power Building	Sunshine Plaza	9:05PM
30	Ngee Ann City	Air View Building	10:40PM
31	Centennial Tower	Ngee Ann City	8:35PM
32	Suntec City Tower	Golden Mile Complex	8:45PM
33	Ministry of Manpower	OUB Center	9:55PM

Table D. 4 (Continued)

Booking Request	Pickup Location	Destination Location	Pickup Time
34	People's Park Complex	Centennial Tower	6:55PM
35	Bank of China	CPF Building	6:55PM
36	OUB Center	Sin Tai Hin Building	8:20PM
37	Air View Building	Ngee Ann City	8:10PM
38	Maxwell Road Food Center	Bugis Village	6:55PM
39	UIC Building	The Paragon Tower	7:50PM
40	CPF Building	Golden Mile Complex	8:40PM
Average Deviation of Pickup Time: $\sum_{i=1}^{n} \mid T_i - \overline{T} \mid /n$			46.4 (min)

Table D. 5 One Set of Randomly Generated Demand with Time Deviations of 59.5 min

Booking Request	Pickup Location	Destination Location	Pickup Time
1	The Paragon Tower	Parco Bugis Junction	9:30 PM
2	Cairnhill Place	Bank of China	9:55 PM
3	Sunshine Plaza	People's Park Complex	11:40 PM
4	Sin Tai Hin Building	Centennial Tower	8:35 PM
5	Parco Bugis Junction	Maxwell Road Food Center	8:25 PM
6	Bugis Village	UIC Building	8:25 PM
7	Golden Mile Complex	Air View Building	7:35 PM
8	Keypoint Building	People's Park Complex	10:30 PM
9	Ngee Ann City	OUB Center	8:25 PM
10	Singapore Power Building	Centennial Tower	6:10 PM
11	Suntec City Tower	Sunshine Plaza	8:50 PM
12	Centennial Tower	Air View Building	7:45 PM
13	People's Park Complex	Ngee Ann City	8:05 PM
14	Ministry of Manpower	Golden Mile Complex	10:00 PM
15	OUB Center	The Paragon Tower	9:45 PM
16	Bank of China	Golden Mile Complex	8:10 PM
17	Maxwell Road Food Center	CPF Building	8:05 PM
18	Air View Building	Sin Tai Hin Building	9:30 PM
19	CPF Building	Ngee Ann City	6:10 PM
20	UIC Building	Bugis Village	8:50 PM
21	Cairnhill Place	People's Park Complex	6:45 PM
22	The Paragon Tower	Centennial Tower	8:50 PM

Table D. 5 (Continued)

Booking Request	Pickup Location	Destination Location	Pickup Time
23	Sunshine Plaza	Air View Building	9:10 PM
24	Sin Tai Hin Building	CPF Building	8:00 PM
25	Parco Bugis Junction	Cairnhill Place	9:40 PM
26	Bugis Village	People's Park Complex	8:00 PM
27	Golden Mile Complex	Parco Bugis Junction	6:30 PM
28	Keypoint Building	Bank of China	10:50 PM
29	Singapore Power Building	Sunshine Plaza	9:05 PM
30	Ngee Ann City	Air View Building	10:40 PM
31	Centennial Tower	Ngee Ann City	8:35 PM
32	Suntec City Tower	Golden Mile Complex	8:45 PM
33	Ministry of Manpower	OUB Center	9:55 PM
34	People's Park Complex	Centennial Tower	6:55 PM
35	Bank of China	CPF Building	6:55 PM
36	OUB Center	Sin Tai Hin Building	8:20 PM
37	Air View Building	Ngee Ann City	8:10 PM
38	Maxwell Road Food Center	Bugis Village	6:55·PM
39	UIC Building	The Paragon Tower	7:50 PM
40	CPF Building	Golden Mile Complex	8:40 PM
Average Deviation of Pickup Time: $\sum_{i=1}^{n} \mid T_i - \overline{T} \mid / n$			59. 5 (min)

Table D. 6 One Set of Randomly Generated Demand with Time Deviations of 64. 1 min

Booking Request	Pickup Location	Destination Location	Pickup Time
1	The Paragon Tower	Parco Bugis Junction	10:05PM
2	Cairnhill Place	Bank of China	8:55PM
3	Sunshine Plaza	People's Park Complex	10:05PM
4	Sin Tai Hin Building	Centennial Tower	8:35PM
5	Parco Bugis Junction	Maxwell Road Food Center	11:25PM
6	Bugis Village	UIC Building	10:40PM
7	Golden Mile Complex	Air View Building	11:25PM
8	Keypoint Building	People's Park Complex	11:15PM
9	Ngee Ann City	OUB Center	8:55PM
10	Singapore Power Building	Centennial Tower	9:25PM
11	Suntec City Tower	Sunshine Plaza	10:25PM

Table D. 6 (Continued)

Booking Request	Pickup Location	Destination Location	Pickup Time
12	Centennial Tower	Air View Building	9:20PM
13	People's Park Complex	Ngee Ann City	9:15PM
14	Ministry of Manpower	Golden Mile Complex	8:50PM
15	OUB Center	The Paragon Tower	7:40PM
16	Bank of China	Golden Mile Complex	8:10PM
17	Maxwell Road Food Center	CPF Building	9:00PM
18	Air View Building	Sin Tai Hin Building	9:20PM
19	CPF Building	Ngee Ann City	7:50PM
20	UIC Building	Bugis Village	7:25PM
21	Cairnhill Place	People's Park Complex	7:00PM
22	The Paragon Tower	Centennial Tower	5:45PM
23	Sunshine Plaza	Air View Building	9:35PM
24	Sin Tai Hin Building	CPF Building	9:30PM
25	Parco Bugis Junction	Cairnhill Place	8:05PM
26	Bugis Village	People's Park Complex	8:55PM
27	Golden Mile Complex	Parco Bugis Junction	6:30PM
28	Keypoint Building	Bank of China	7:30PM
29	Singapore Power Building	Sunshine Plaza	11:55PM
30	Ngee Ann City	Air View Building	8:20PM
31	Centennial Tower	Ngee Ann City	8:50PM
32	Suntec City Tower	Golden Mile Complex	10:05PM
33	Ministry of Manpower	OUB Center	7:05PM
34	People's Park Complex	Centennial Tower	10:05PM
35	Bank of China	CPF Building	7:15PM
36	OUB Center	Sin Tai Hin Building	8:35PM
37	Air View Building	Ngee Ann City	9:05PM
38	Maxwell Road Food Center	Bugis Village	9:10PM
39	UIC Building	The Paragon Tower	7:45PM
40	CPF Building	Golden Mile Complex	9:35PM
Average Deviation of Pickup Time: $\sum_{i=1}^{n} \mid T_i - \overline{T} \mid /n$			64.1 (min)

Table D. 7 One Set of Randomly Generated Demand with Time Deviations of 74. 5 min

Booking Request	Pickup Location	Destination Location	Pickup Time
1	The Paragon Tower	Parco Bugis Junction	5:50PM
2	Cairnhill Place	Bank of China	11:20PM
3	Sunshine Plaza	People's Park Complex	8:05PM
4	Sin Tai Hin Building	Centennial Tower	9:10PM
5	Parco Bugis Junction	Maxwell Road Food Center	8:25PM
6	Bugis Village	UIC Building	10:05PM
7	Golden Mile Complex	Air View Building	9:10PM
8	Keypoint Building	People's Park Complex	9:20PM
9	Ngee Ann City	OUB Center	9:25PM
10	Singapore Power Building	Centennial Tower	6:45PM
11	Suntec City Tower	Sunshine Plaza	7:55PM
12	Centennial Tower	Air View Building	10:35PM
13	People's Park Complex	Ngee Ann City	11:25PM
14	Ministry of Manpower	Golden Mile Complex	9:10PM
15	OUB Center	The Paragon Tower	10:50PM
16	Bank of China	Golden Mile Complex	10:45PM
17	Maxwell Road Food Center	CPF Building	11:40PM
18	Air View Building	Sin Tai Hin Building	10:30PM
19	CPF Building	Ngee Ann City	6:45PM
20	UIC Building	Bugis Village	9:35PM
21	Cairnhill Place	People's Park Complex	8:50PM
22	The Paragon Tower	Centennial Tower	11:00PM
23	Sunshine Plaza	Air View Building	10:55PM
24	Sin Tai Hin Building	CPF Building	10:15PM
25	Parco Bugis Junction	Cairnhill Place	10:00PM
26	Bugis Village	People's Park Complex	9:30PM
27	Golden Mile Complex	Parco Bugis Junction	8:05PM
28	Keypoint Building	Bank of China	11:15PM
29	Singapore Power Building	Sunshine Plaza	11:55PM
30	Ngee Ann City	Air View Building	9:00PM
31	Centennial Tower	Ngee Ann City	7:05PM
32	Suntec City Tower	Golden Mile Complex	9:25PM
33	Ministry of Manpower	OUB Center	9:55PM

Table D. 7 (Continued)

Booking Request	Pickup Location	Destination Location	Pickup Time
34	People's Park Complex	Centennial Tower	9:40PM
35	Bank of China	CPF Building	11:45PM
36	OUB Center	Sin Tai Hin Building	9:10PM
37	Air View Building	Ngee Ann City	7:15PM
38	Maxwell Road Food Center	Bugis Village	8:50PM
39	UIC Building	The Paragon Tower	6:50PM
40	CPF Building	Golden Mile Complex	11:15PM
Average Deviation of Pickup Time: $\sum_{i=1}^{n} \mid T_i - \overline{T} \mid / n$			74. 5 (min)

Table D. 8 One Set of Randomly Generated Demand with Time Deviations of 88. 4 min

Booking Request	Pickup Location	Destination Location	Pickup Time
1	The Paragon Tower	Parco Bugis Junction	8:20PM
2	Cairnhill Place	Bank of China	7:00PM
3	Sunshine Plaza	People's Park Complex	9:15PM
4	Sin Tai Hin Building	Centennial Tower	9:00PM
5	Parco Bugis Junction	Maxwell Road Food Center	9:35PM
6	Bugis Village	UIC Building	6:30PM
7	Golden Mile Complex	Air View Building	8:45PM
8	Keypoint Building	People's Park Complex	11:50PM
9	Ngee Ann City	OUB Center	10:00PM
10	Singapore Power Building	Centennial Tower	11:35PM
11	Suntec City Tower	Sunshine Plaza	6:45PM
12	Centennial Tower	Air View Building	7:40PM
13	People's Park Complex	Ngee Ann City	6:40PM
14	Ministry of Manpower	Golden Mile Complex	12:00PM
15	OUB Center	The Paragon Tower	8:30PM
16	Bank of China	Golden Mile Complex	12:00PM
17	Maxwell Road Food Center	CPF Building	6:05PM
18	Air View Building	Sin Tai Hin Building	9:35PM
19	CPF Building	Ngee Ann City	6:05PM
20	UIC Building	Bugis Village	8:20PM
21	Cairnhill Place	People's Park Complex	11:35PM
22	The Paragon Tower	Centennial Tower	5:45PM

Table D. 8 (Continued)

Booking Request	Pickup Location	Destination Location	Pickup Time
23	Sunshine Plaza	Air View Building	11:20PM
24	Sin Tai Hin Building	CPF Building	7:20PM
25	Parco Bugis Junction	Cairnhill Place	6:55PM
26	Bugis Village	People's Park Complex	10:30PM
27	Golden Mile Complex	Parco Bugis Junction	8:10PM
28	Keypoint Building	Bank of China	6:45PM
29	Singapore Power Building	Sunshine Plaza	9:35PM
30	Ngee Ann City	Air View Building	9:25PM
31	Centennial Tower	Ngee Ann City	8:25PM
32	Suntec City Tower	Golden Mile Complex	8:30PM
33	Ministry of Manpower	OUB Center	9:25PM
34	People's Park Complex	Centennial Tower	9:40PM
35	Bank of China	CPF Building	11:05PM
36	OUB Center	Sin Tai Hin Building	10:55PM
37	Air View Building	Ngee Ann City	9:35PM
38	Maxwell Road Food Center	Bugis Village	10:10PM
39	UIC Building	The Paragon Tower	9:10PM
40	CPF Building	Golden Mile Complex	7:55PM
Average Deviation of Pickup Time: $\sum_{i=1}^{n} \mid T_i - \bar{T} \mid / n$			88.4 (min)

Table D. 9 One Set of Randomly Generated Demand with Time Deviations of 94.7 min

Booking Request	Pickup Location	Destination Location	Pickup Time
1	The Paragon Tower	Parco Bugis Junction	5:30PM
2	Cairnhill Place	Bank of China	9:10PM
3	Sunshine Plaza	People's Park Complex	6:45PM
4	Sin Tai Hin Building	Centennial Tower	10:45PM
5	Parco Bugis Junction	Maxwell Road Food Center	9:20PM
6	Bugis Village	UIC Building	8:35PM
7	Golden Mile Complex	Air View Building	7:45PM
8	Keypoint Building	People's Park Complex	11:20PM
9	Ngee Ann City	OUB Center	10:55PM
10	Singapore Power Building	Centennial Tower	10:20PM
11	Suntec City Tower	Sunshine Plaza	6:35PM

Table D. 9 (Continued)

Booking Request	Pickup Location	Destination Location	Pickup Time
12	Centennial Tower	Air View Building	11:05PM
13	People's Park Complex	Ngee Ann City	10:10PM
14	Ministry of Manpower	Golden Mile Complex	8:50PM
15	OUB Center	The Paragon Tower	7:30PM
16	Bank of China	Golden Mile Complex	5:35PM
17	Maxwell Road Food Center	CPF Building	6:05PM
18	Air View Building	Sin Tai Hin Building	7:50PM
19	CPF Building	Ngee Ann City	6:25PM
20	UIC Building	Bugis Village	6:35PM
21	Cairnhill Place	People's Park Complex	12:00PM
22	The Paragon Tower	Centennial Tower	8:25PM
23	Sunshine Plaza	Air View Building	6:15PM
24	Sin Tai Hin Building	CPF Building	5:30PM
25	Parco Bugis Junction	Cairnhill Place	5:30PM
26	Bugis Village	People's Park Complex	7:55PM
27	Golden Mile Complex	Parco Bugis Junction	9:00PM
28	Keypoint Building	Bank of China	9:15PM
29	Singapore Power Building	Sunshine Plaza	9:25PM
30	Ngee Ann City	Air View Building	9:25PM
31	Centennial Tower	Ngee Ann City	6:35PM
32	Suntec City Tower	Golden Mile Complex	9:50PM
33	Ministry of Manpower	OUB Center	8:25PM
34	People's Park Complex	Centennial Tower	7:45PM
35	Bank of China	CPF Building	5:50PM
36	OUB Center	Sin Tai Hin Building	9:30PM
37	Air View Building	Ngee Ann City	10:35PM
38	Maxwell Road Food Center	Bugis Village	10:45PM
39	UIC Building	The Paragon Tower	8:55PM
40	CPF Building	Golden Mile Complex	7:25PM
Average Deviation of Pickup Time: $\sum_{i=1}^{n} \mid T_i - \overline{T} \mid / n$			94.7 (min)

Table D. 10 One Set of Randomly Generated Demand with Time Deviations of 107. 6 min

Booking Request	Pickup Location	Destination Location	Pickup Time
1	The Paragon Tower	Parco Bugis Junction	11:15PM
2	Cairnhill Place	Bank of China	10:15PM
3	Sunshine Plaza	People's Park Complex	11:45PM
4	Sin Tai Hin Building	Centennial Tower	11:35PM
5	Parco Bugis Junction	Maxwell Road Food Center	9:00PM
6	Bugis Village	UIC Building	6:25PM
7	Golden Mile Complex	Air View Building	8:30PM
8	Keypoint Building	People's Park Complex	7:00PM
9	Ngee Ann City	OUB Center	11:10PM
10	Singapore Power Building	Centennial Tower	6:50PM
11	Suntec City Tower	Sunshine Plaza	10:35PM
12	Centennial Tower	Air View Building	11:00PM
13	People's Park Complex	Ngee Ann City	12:00PM
14	Ministry of Manpower	Golden Mile Complex	12:00PM
15	OUB Center	The Paragon Tower	9:30PM
16	Bank of China	Golden Mile Complex	8:05PM
17	Maxwell Road Food Center	CPF Building	7:15PM
18	Air View Building	Sin Tai Hin Building	7:25PM
19	CPF Building	Ngee Ann City	11:00PM
20	UIC Building	Bugis Village	5:35PM
21	Cairnhill Place	People's Park Complex	7:55PM
22	The Paragon Tower	Centennial Tower	6:05PM
23	Sunshine Plaza	Air View Building	9:55PM
24	Sin Tai Hin Building	CPF Building	5:50PM
25	Parco Bugis Junction	Cairnhill Place	5:30PM
26	Bugis Village	People's Park Complex	11:30PM
27	Golden Mile Complex	Parco Bugis Junction	7:15PM
28	Keypoint Building	Bank of China	7:15PM
29	Singapore Power Building	Sunshine Plaza	9:20PM
30	Ngee Ann City	Air View Building	10:00PM
31	Centennial Tower	Ngee Ann City	11:00PM
32	Suntec City Tower	Golden Mile Complex	10:15PM
33	Ministry of Manpower	OUB Center	8:40PM

Table D. 10(Continued)

Booking Request	Pickup Location	Destination Location	Pickup Time
34	People's Park Complex	Centennial Tower	6:50PM
35	Bank of China	CPF Building	10:20PM
36	OUB Center	Sin Tai Hin Building	8:35PM
37	Air View Building	Ngee Ann City	8:30PM
38	Maxwell Road Food Center	Bugis Village	11:40PM
39	UIC Building	The Paragon Tower	10:20PM
40	CPF Building	Golden Mile Complex	6:10PM
	Average Deviation of Pickup Time: $\sum_{i=1}^{n} \mid T_i - \overline{T} \mid /n$		107.6 (min)

Table D. 11 One Set of Randomly Generated Demand with Time Deviations of 111.5 min

Booking Request	Pickup Location	Destination Location	Pickup Time
1	The Paragon Tower	Parco Bugis Junction	9:00PM
2	Cairnhill Place	Bank of China	11:55PM
3	Sunshine Plaza	People's Park Complex	5:50PM
4	Sin Tai Hin Building	Centennial Tower	6:00PM
5	Parco Bugis Junction	Maxwell Road Food Center	8:55PM
6	Bugis Village	UIC Building	8:15PM
7	Golden Mile Complex	Air View Building	6:05PM
8	Keypoint Building	People's Park Complex	7:10PM
9	Ngee Ann City	OUB Center	11:20PM
10	Singapore Power Building	Centennial Tower	7:00PM
11	Suntec City Tower	Sunshine Plaza	6:25PM
12	Centennial Tower	Air View Building	6:15PM
13	People's Park Complex	Ngee Ann City	11:35PM
14	Ministry of Manpower	Golden Mile Complex	6:00PM
15	OUB Center	The Paragon Tower	5:45PM
16	Bank of China	Golden Mile Complex	5:50PM
17	Maxwell Road Food Center	CPF Building	7:40PM
18	Air View Building	Sin Tai Hin Building	11:30PM
19	CPF Building	Ngee Ann City	8:05PM
20	UIC Building	Bugis Village	8:20PM
21	Cairnhill Place	People's Park Complex	11:40PM
22	The Paragon Tower	Centennial Tower	11:00PM

Table D. 11 (Continued)

Booking Request	Pickup Location	Destination Location	Pickup Time
23	Sunshine Plaza	Air View Building	9:00PM
24	Sin Tai Hin Building	CPF Building	11:00PM
25	Parco Bugis Junction	Cairnhill Place	10:00PM
26	Bugis Village	People's Park Complex	8:05PM
27	Golden Mile Complex	Parco Bugis Junction	7:10PM
28	Keypoint Building	Bank of China	5:30PM
29	Singapore Power Building	Sunshine Plaza	8:55PM
30	Ngee Ann City	Air View Building	11:45PM
31	Centennial Tower	Ngee Ann City	8:05PM
32	Suntec City Tower	Golden Mile Complex	7:05PM
33	Ministry of Manpower	OUB Center	9:20PM
34	People's Park Complex	Centennial Tower	7:10PM
35	Bank of China	CPF Building	10:00PM
36	OUB Center	Sin Tai Hin Building	11:40PM
37	Air View Building	Ngee Ann City	8:20PM
38	Maxwell Road Food Center	Bugis Village	11:20PM
39	UIC Building	The Paragon Tower	5:30PM
40	CPF Building	Golden Mile Complex	11:40PM
Average Deviation of Pickup Time: $\sum_{i=1}^{n} \mid T_i - \overline{T} \mid /n$			111.5 (min)

Table D. 12 One Set of Randomly Generated Demand with Time Deviations of 123.9 min

Booking Request	Pickup Location	Destination Location	Pickup Time
1	The Paragon Tower	Parco Bugis Junction	6:30PM
2	Cairnhill Place	Bank of China	8:15PM
3	Sunshine Plaza	People's Park Complex	5:45PM
4	Sin Tai Hin Building	Centennial Tower	10:50PM
5	Parco Bugis Junction	Maxwell Road Food Center	7:10PM
6	Bugis Village	UIC Building	6:25PM
7	Golden Mile Complex	Air View Building	5:40PM
8	Keypoint Building	People's Park Complex	10:20PM
9	Ngee Ann City	OUB Center	10:40PM
10	Singapore Power Building	Centennial Tower	9:50PM
11	Suntec City Tower	Sunshine Plaza	11:50PM

Table D. 12(Continued)

Booking Request	Pickup Location	Destination Location	Pickup Time
12	Centennial Tower	Air View Building	10:50PM
13	People's Park Complex	Ngee Ann City	10:55PM
14	Ministry of Manpower	Golden Mile Complex	6:10PM
15	OUB Center	The Paragon Tower	11:45PM
16	Bank of China	Golden Mile Complex	10:45PM
17	Maxwell Road Food Center	CPF Building	7:55PM
18	Air View Building	Sin Tai Hin Building	5:55PM
19	CPF Building	Ngee Ann City	5:35PM
20	UIC Building	Bugis Village	10:05PM
21	Cairnhill Place	People's Park Complex	9:30PM
22	The Paragon Tower	Centennial Tower	11:05PM
23	Sunshine Plaza	Air View Building	11:55PM
24	Sin Tai Hin Building	CPF Building	7:35PM
25	Parco Bugis Junction	Cairnhill Place	11:20PM
26	Bugis Village	People's Park Complex	11:00PM
27	Golden Mile Complex	Parco Bugis Junction	5:40PM
28	Keypoint Building	Bank of China	9:40PM
29	Singapore Power Building	Sunshine Plaza	5:40PM
30	Ngee Ann City	Air View Building	9:20PM
31	Centennial Tower	Ngee Ann City	5:35PM
32	Suntec City Tower	Golden Mile Complex	6:05PM
33	Ministry of Manpower	OUB Center	7:45PM
34	People's Park Complex	Centennial Tower	10:50PM
35	Bank of China	CPF Building	5:45PM
36	OUB Center	Sin Tai Hin Building	11:15PM
37	Air View Building	Ngee Ann City	6:50PM
38	Maxwell Road Food Center	Bugis Village	5:50PM
39	UIC Building	The Paragon Tower	7:45PM
40	CPF Building	Golden Mile Complex	8:25PM
Average Deviation of Pickup Time: $\sum_{i=1}^{n} \mid T_i - \overline{T} \mid / n$			123.9 (min)

Appendix E: Details of the Routing Solutions

E-1. Output File for Improved Solutions (Heuristics Based on Nearest Neighbor Insertion with TABU Search)

* * The demand was sorted according to the pickup time sequence before calculation.

```
======Pickup time deviation is 15.05=====================
Total cost:  282.777 (in Min)
============================================================
  1, route_cost =   38.2,n_demand =   6:   5, 15, 19, 28, 31, 36,
  2, route_cost =   42.9,n_demand =   6:   2,  6, 13, 24, 33, 39,
  3, route_cost =   42.0,n_demand =   6:   7, 14, 18, 22, 30, 35,
  4, route_cost =   38.4,n_demand =   5:   3, 16, 23, 32, 40,
  5, route_cost =   33.6,n_demand =   5:   4, 12, 20, 29, 38,
  6, route_cost =   30.7,n_demand =   4:   1,  8, 25, 37,
  7, route_cost =   31.5,n_demand =   4:  11, 21, 26, 34,
  8, route_cost =   18.8,n_demand =   3:   9, 17, 27,
  9, route_cost =    6.7,n_demand =   1:  10,

======Pickup time deviation is 23.64=====================
Total cost:  279.375 (in Min)
============================================================
  1, route_cost =   64.2,n_demand =  10:   2,  7, 14, 25, 27, 32, 33, 35, 37, 39,
  2, route_cost =   44.2,n_demand =   7:   3, 12, 18, 29, 34, 36, 38,
  3, route_cost =   51.1,n_demand =   7:   1, 10, 16, 19, 23, 30, 40,
  4, route_cost =   37.5,n_demand =   5:   6, 15, 21, 24, 31,
  5, route_cost =   34.7,n_demand =   5:   8, 11, 17, 22, 28,
  6, route_cost =   35.6,n_demand =   4:   4,  9, 20, 26,
  7, route_cost =   12.2,n_demand =   2:   5, 13,
======Pickup time deviation is 30.55=====================
Total cost:  288.042 (in Min)
============================================================
  1, route_cost =   73.4,n_demand =  10:   1,  6, 10, 14, 18, 23, 25, 30, 39, 40,
  2, route_cost =   56.8,n_demand =   8:   2,  5,  9, 15, 21, 27, 33, 35,
```

```
 3, route_cost =   57.0,n_demand =  8:   8, 11, 20, 22, 29, 32, 34, 36,
 4, route_cost =   42.3,n_demand =  6:   7, 16, 19, 24, 28, 31,
 5, route_cost =   40.7,n_demand =  6:   4, 13, 17, 26, 37, 38,
 6, route_cost =   17.9,n_demand =  2:   3, 12,

======Pickup time deviation is 46.38=====================
Total cost:  279.917 (in Min)
==================================================================
 1, route_cost =   62.0,n_demand = 10:   5,  7,  9, 15, 19, 22, 23, 25, 28, 31,
 2, route_cost =   64.9,n_demand =  9:   6, 14, 17, 21, 26, 29, 32, 36, 37,
 3, route_cost =   56.9,n_demand =  9:   1,  3, 10, 11, 20, 24, 34, 39, 40,
 4, route_cost =   76.4,n_demand =  9:   2,  4, 13, 18, 27, 30, 33, 35, 38,
 5, route_cost =   19.8,n_demand =  3:   8, 12, 16,

======Pickup time deviation is 59.50=====================
Total cost:  295.495 (in Min)
==================================================================
 1, route_cost =   94.4,n_demand = 13:   1,  3,  7,  9, 13, 17, 24, 29, 32, 35, 38, 39,
40,
 2, route_cost =   82.3,n_demand = 11:   2,  8, 11, 16, 19, 25, 28, 30, 33, 36, 37,
 3, route_cost =   75.8,n_demand = 10:   4,  6, 10, 14, 18, 22, 23, 26, 31, 34,
 4, route_cost =   43.1,n_demand =  6:   5, 12, 15, 20, 21, 27,

======Pickup time deviation is 64.13=====================
Total cost:  269.062 (in Min)
==================================================================
 1, route_cost =   80.2,n_demand = 11:   4,  7, 11, 13, 19, 22, 26, 29, 31, 35, 39,
 2, route_cost =   71.1,n_demand = 11:   2,  3, 10, 12, 14, 18, 24, 27, 30, 34, 38,
 3, route_cost =   52.7,n_demand =  8:   1,  5,  6, 17, 32, 36, 37, 40,
 4, route_cost =   57.8,n_demand =  8:   9, 15, 16, 21, 23, 25, 28, 33,
 5, route_cost =    7.2,n_demand =  2:   8, 20,

======Pickup time deviation is 74.50=====================
Total cost:  277.923 (in Min)
==================================================================
 1, route_cost =   95.2,n_demand = 13:   1,  4,  7,  9, 14, 19, 23, 25, 28, 32, 36, 38,
40,
 2, route_cost =   88.2,n_demand = 12:   2,  8, 11, 13, 15, 18, 21, 29, 30, 34, 37, 39,
```

```
  3, route_cost =   74.9,n_demand = 12:   5,  6, 12, 17, 20, 22, 24, 26, 27, 31, 33, 35,
  4, route_cost =   19.6,n_demand =  3:   3, 10, 16,

 =====Pickup time deviation is 88.43 ====================
Total cost:  267.697 (in Min)
 ==========================================================
  1, route_cost =   68.4,n_demand = 10:   7, 10, 11, 12, 18, 20, 22, 23, 25, 35,
  2, route_cost =   68.6,n_demand =  9:   2,  4,  6, 14, 19, 28, 34, 37, 40,
  3, route_cost =   58.5,n_demand =  9:   5,  9, 16, 21, 24, 26, 30, 33, 39,
  4, route_cost =   46.8,n_demand =  8:   3, 13, 17, 27, 31, 32, 36, 38,
  5, route_cost =   25.4,n_demand =  4:   1,  8, 15, 29,

 ======Pickup time deviation is 94.70 ====================
Total cost:  280.913 (in Min)
 ==========================================================
  1, route_cost = 118.1,n_demand = 17:   1,  5,  8,  9, 12, 13, 15, 18, 19, 23, 25, 29,
32, 33, 36, 39, 40,
  2, route_cost = 105.3,n_demand = 15:   3,  6, 10, 14, 16, 21, 22, 24, 26, 28, 31, 34, 35,
37, 38,
  3, route_cost =   57.5,n_demand =  8:   2,  4,  7, 11, 17, 20, 27, 30,

 ======Pickup time deviation is 107.63 ====================
Total cost:  288.280 (in Min)
 ==========================================================
  1, route_cost =   99.2,n_demand = 14:   2,  3,  4,  7,  9, 16, 20, 22, 23, 28, 32, 33,
37, 39,
  2, route_cost =   96.1,n_demand = 13:   5,  6,  8, 12, 13, 15, 18, 24, 26, 31, 35, 38,
40,
  3, route_cost =   63.9,n_demand =  9:  10, 14, 17, 19, 25, 29, 30, 34, 36,
  4, route_cost =   29.1,n_demand =  4:   1, 11, 21, 27,

 =====Pickup time deviation is 111.47 ====================
Total cost:  306.848 (in Min)
 ==========================================================
  1, route_cost =   99.1,n_demand = 12:   1,  4,  7, 11, 15, 18, 22, 23, 28, 34, 37, 40,
```

```
2, route_cost =   87.3,n_demand = 11:   6,  9, 10, 14, 17, 20, 25, 29, 30, 33, 36,
3, route_cost =   56.0,n_demand =  9:   3,  5, 13, 16, 19, 24, 31, 35, 39,
4, route_cost =   64.4,n_demand =  8:   2,  8, 12, 21, 26, 27, 32, 38,

======Pickup time deviation is 123.90 ======================
Total cost:  293.393 (in Min)
===========================================================
1, route_cost =   67.6,n_demand =  9:   5,  9, 13, 15, 18, 20, 22, 29, 34,
2, route_cost =   57.2,n_demand =  9:   3,  7, 10, 12, 14, 31, 36, 38, 39,
3, route_cost =   61.5,n_demand =  8:   1,  8, 11, 19, 24, 33, 37, 40,
4, route_cost =   65.2,n_demand =  8:   2,  6, 16, 25, 27, 28, 32, 35,
5, route_cost =   41.9,n_demand =  6:   4, 17, 21, 23, 26, 30,
```

E-2. Output File for Improved Solutions (Heuristics Based on Sweep Insertion with TABU Search)

* * The demand was sorted according to the pickup time sequence before calculation.

```
======Pickup time deviation is 15.05 ======================
Total cost:  273.525 (in Min)
===========================================================
1, route_cost =   38.1,n_demand =  6:   2,  4,  9, 24, 33, 40,
2, route_cost =   42.3,n_demand =  6:   1,  3, 16, 19, 29, 37,
3, route_cost =   33.2,n_demand =  5:   5, 12, 18, 22, 35,
4, route_cost =   33.8,n_demand =  5:   8, 17, 26, 32, 39,
5, route_cost =   30.6,n_demand =  5:   7, 13, 21, 27, 31,
6, route_cost =   30.8,n_demand =  4:  10, 23, 30, 36,
7, route_cost =   34.0,n_demand =  4:   6, 14, 25, 34,
8, route_cost =   23.9,n_demand =  4:  15, 20, 28, 38,
9, route_cost =    6.9,n_demand =  1:  11,

======Pickup time deviation is 23.64 ======================
Total cost:  285.247 (in Min)
===========================================================
1, route_cost =   73.3,n_demand = 10:   2,  9, 14, 18, 25, 27, 31, 36, 38, 39,
2, route_cost =   62.5,n_demand =  9:   1, 10, 16, 19, 24, 30, 35, 37, 40,
3, route_cost =   43.1,n_demand =  6:   4,  8, 13, 22, 32, 33,
```

```
  4, route_cost =   27.9,n_demand =   5:   3, 15, 20, 29, 34,
  5, route_cost =   43.0,n_demand =   5:   5,  7, 17, 23, 28,
  6, route_cost =   28.8,n_demand =   4:   6, 11, 21, 26,
  7, route_cost =    6.7,n_demand =   1:  12,

======Pickup time deviation is 30.55 =====================
Total cost:  286.915 (in Min)
==================================================================
  1, route_cost =   54.6,n_demand =   8:   3,  9, 15, 18, 27, 33, 35, 39,
  2, route_cost =   57.5,n_demand =   8:   2, 12, 19, 23, 25, 30, 37, 38,
  3, route_cost =   53.6,n_demand =   8:   4, 16, 20, 24, 29, 32, 34, 36,
  4, route_cost =   59.0,n_demand =   7:   5, 10, 14, 21, 26, 31, 40,
  5, route_cost =   50.2,n_demand =   7:   1,  6,  8, 13, 17, 22, 28,
  6, route_cost =   11.9,n_demand =   2:   7, 11,

======Pickup time deviation is 46.38 =====================
  the initial route (sweep insert heuristics)   total cost:  279.007 (in Min)
==================================================================
  1, route_cost =   76.6,n_demand = 11:   3,  7, 10, 11, 20, 21, 26, 29, 32, 36, 38,
  2, route_cost =   71.1,n_demand = 10:   1,  5, 13, 18, 22, 24, 28, 33, 39, 40,
  3, route_cost =   59.6,n_demand =  9:   4, 12, 16, 19, 23, 25, 30, 34, 35,
  4, route_cost =   59.7,n_demand =  8:   2,  6,  8, 14, 17, 27, 31, 37,
  5, route_cost =   11.9,n_demand =  2:   9, 15,

======Pickup time deviation is 59.50 =====================
Total cost:  279.657 (in Min)
==================================================================
  1, route_cost =   89.2,n_demand = 13:   1,  3,  7,  9, 11, 15, 20, 21, 27, 32, 35, 38,
40,
  2, route_cost =   69.4,n_demand = 11:   4,  5, 12, 14, 18, 24, 28, 30, 33, 36, 39,
  3, route_cost =   83.6,n_demand = 11:   6, 10, 13, 17, 22, 23, 26, 29, 31, 34, 37,
  4, route_cost =   37.6,n_demand =  5:   2,  8, 16, 19, 25,

======Pickup time deviation is 64.13 =====================
Total cost:  281.910 (in Min)
==================================================================
  1, route_cost =   70.7,n_demand = 11:   2,  3, 10, 11, 19, 23, 27, 30, 34, 37, 38,
```

```
  2, route_cost =   74.2,n_demand = 10:   1,  5,  6,  8, 20, 24, 32, 36, 39, 40,
  3, route_cost =   64.5,n_demand =  9:   4,  7, 14, 17, 22, 25, 29, 33, 35,
  4, route_cost =   53.7,n_demand =  7:   9, 15, 16, 21, 26, 28, 31,
  5, route_cost =   18.9,n_demand =  3:  12, 13, 18,

======Pickup time deviation is 74.50======================
Total cost:  308.192 (in Min)
==============================================================
  1, route_cost = 114.1,n_demand = 15:   1,  4,  7,  9, 10, 11, 17, 19, 25, 27, 31, 32,
35, 38, 40,
  2, route_cost =   81.4,n_demand = 11:   2,  8, 15, 18, 21, 23, 26, 29, 34, 37, 39,
  3, route_cost =   91.6,n_demand = 11:   3,  6, 13, 14, 20, 22, 24, 28, 30, 33, 36,
  4, route_cost =   21.1,n_demand =  3:   5, 12, 16,

======Pickup time deviation is 88.43======================
Total cost:  288.800 (in Min)
==============================================================
  1, route_cost =   92.6,n_demand = 12:   2,  4,  6, 12, 14, 18, 19, 29, 31, 34, 37, 39,
  2, route_cost =   60.8,n_demand =  9:   5,  9, 15, 17, 24, 26, 30, 33, 40,
  3, route_cost =   66.5,n_demand =  9:   1, 13, 16, 21, 23, 28, 32, 36, 38,
  4, route_cost =   51.4,n_demand =  7:   7, 10, 11, 20, 22, 25, 35,
  5, route_cost =   17.5,n_demand =  3:  3,  8, 27,

======Pickup time deviation is 94.70======================
Total cost:  282.495 (in Min)
==============================================================
  1, route_cost = 120.9,n_demand = 17:   3,  6,  7, 10, 13, 15, 18, 20, 23, 25, 29, 32,
33, 36, 37, 38, 39,
  2, route_cost = 100.6,n_demand = 14:   1,  5,  8, 11, 16, 21, 22, 24, 26, 28, 31, 34,
35, 40,
  3, route_cost =   60.9,n_demand =  9:   2,  4,  9, 12, 14, 17, 19, 27, 30,

======Pickup time deviation is 107.63======================
Total cost:  285.073 (in Min)
==============================================================
  1, route_cost =   86.0,n_demand = 14:   5,  6,  8, 12, 13, 14, 17, 19, 22, 23, 26, 30,
```

```
37, 40,
  2, route_cost =   94.6,n_demand = 13:   2,  3,  4,  7,  9, 16, 20, 28, 32, 33, 35, 38,
39,
  3, route_cost =   79.5,n_demand =  9:  10, 15, 18, 21, 27, 29, 31, 34, 36,
  4, route_cost =   24.9,n_demand =  4:   1, 11, 24, 25,


=====Pickup time deviation is 111.47 ====================
Total cost:  288.648 (in Min)
==========================================================
  1, route_cost =   52.8,n_demand =  9:   5,  7, 13, 19, 21, 24, 31, 35, 40,
  2, route_cost =   57.2,n_demand =  9:   9, 12, 18, 20, 25, 27, 29, 34, 37,
  3, route_cost =   78.4,n_demand =  9:   2,  4,  6, 14, 16, 23, 30, 32, 36,
  4, route_cost =   53.0,n_demand =  7:   3,  8, 10, 11, 26, 33, 39,
  5, route_cost =   47.2,n_demand =  6:   1, 15, 17, 22, 28, 38,


=====Pickup time deviation is 123.90 ====================
Total cost:  296.123 (in Min)
==========================================================
  1, route_cost =  106.8,n_demand = 14:   2,  6, 10, 15, 18, 19, 20, 22, 27, 29, 33, 37, 38,
40,
  2, route_cost =   75.4,n_demand = 10:   3,  7,  9, 12, 24, 25, 28, 32, 35, 36,
  3, route_cost =   62.0,n_demand =  9:   4, 16, 17, 21, 23, 26, 30, 34, 39,
  4, route_cost =   52.0,n_demand =  7:   1,  5,  8, 11, 13, 14, 31,
```

E-3. Output File for Improved Solutions (Heuristics Based on Earliest Time Insertion with TABU Search)

* * The demand was sorted according to the pickup time sequence before calculation.

```
=====Pickup time deviation is 15.05 ====================
Total cost:  267.220 (in Min)
==========================================================
  1, route_cost =   55.1,n_demand =  8:   1,  5, 15, 18, 22, 30, 36, 40,
  2, route_cost =   45.8,n_demand =  7:   2,  4,  9, 17, 23, 32, 39,
  3, route_cost =   38.3,n_demand =  5:   7, 13, 21, 26, 35,
  4, route_cost =   28.8,n_demand =  5:  10, 19, 28, 31, 38,
```

```
  5, route_cost =   27.8,n_demand =   4:  16, 20, 25, 34,
  6, route_cost =   28.5,n_demand =   4:   6, 14, 24, 33,
  7, route_cost =   27.6,n_demand =   4:   3, 12, 29, 37,
  8, route_cost =    8.4,n_demand =   2:   8, 27,
  9, route_cost =    6.9,n_demand =   1:  11,


======Pickup time deviation is 23.64 =====================
Total cost:  275.388 (in Min)
=============================================================
  1, route_cost =   88.5,n_demand = 12:   3,  5,  7, 14, 18, 23, 28, 34, 36, 38, 39, 40,
  2, route_cost =   65.6,n_demand =  9:   2,  6, 13, 17, 22, 26, 30, 35, 37,
  3, route_cost =   49.3,n_demand =  7:   4,  8, 11, 19, 25, 27, 31,
  4, route_cost =   35.7,n_demand =  6:   1, 16, 20, 24, 29, 33,
  5, route_cost =   23.1,n_demand =  4:  10, 15, 21, 32,
  6, route_cost =    6.4,n_demand =  1:   9,
  7, route_cost =    6.7,n_demand =  1:  12,


======Pickup time deviation is 30.55 =====================
Total cost:  283.253 (in Min)
=============================================================
  1, route_cost =  118.6,n_demand = 17:   1,  2,  3,  4,  6,  8, 13, 17, 21, 24, 28, 31,
33, 35, 37, 38, 40,
  2, route_cost =   79.3,n_demand = 10:   5, 10, 14, 18, 22, 29, 32, 34, 36, 39,
  3, route_cost =   42.0,n_demand =  6:   7, 11, 20, 23, 25, 30,
  4, route_cost =   18.2,n_demand =  3:  15, 19, 26,
  5, route_cost =   18.4,n_demand =  3:   9, 16, 27,
  6, route_cost =    6.7,n_demand =  1:  12,


======Pickup time deviation is 46.38 =====================
Total cost:  283.015 (in Min)
=============================================================
  1, route_cost =  123.2,n_demand = 17:   1,  2,  4,  6,  7,  9, 14, 17, 21, 25, 28, 29,
32, 35, 38, 39, 40,
  2, route_cost =   84.4,n_demand = 11:   3,  8, 15, 19, 22, 23, 27, 30, 34, 36, 37,
  3, route_cost =   35.3,n_demand =  6:   5, 10, 11, 18, 24, 31,
```

4, route_cost = 33.3, n_demand = 5: 12, 16, 20, 26, 33,

5, route_cost = 6.7, n_demand = 1: 13,

======Pickup time deviation is 59.50======================

Total cost: 288.042 (in Min)

==

1, route_cost = 149.8, n_demand = 19: 2, 3, 4, 6, 8, 9, 11, 15, 17, 21, 25, 28, 30, 32, 35, 37, 38, 39, 40,

2, route_cost = 82.8, n_demand = 12: 1, 7, 10, 13, 19, 22, 23, 26, 29, 31, 33, 36,

3, route_cost = 35.8, n_demand = 6: 5, 12, 14, 18, 24, 34,

4, route_cost = 19.6, n_demand = 3: 16, 20, 27,

======Pickup time deviation is 64.13======================

Total cost: 279.028 (in Min)

==

1, route_cost = 143.5, n_demand = 21: 1, 2, 4, 5, 7, 8, 10, 12, 13, 14, 16, 21, 23, 25, 28, 31, 35, 36, 37, 38, 40,

2, route_cost = 84.9, n_demand = 11: 3, 6, 9, 11, 15, 17, 22, 26, 29, 33, 39,

3, route_cost = 32.8, n_demand = 5: 18, 24, 27, 30, 34,

4, route_cost = 13.4, n_demand = 2: 19, 32,

5, route_cost = 4.4, n_demand = 1: 20,

======Pickup time deviation is 74.50======================

Total cost: 274.630 (in Min)

==

1, route_cost = 161.3, n_demand = 23: 1, 2, 5, 6, 7, 9, 10, 11, 13, 15, 18, 21, 23, 24, 26, 27, 29, 30, 33, 35, 37, 38, 40,

2, route_cost = 80.7, n_demand = 12: 3, 8, 12, 17, 20, 22, 25, 28, 31, 32, 36, 39,

3, route_cost = 26.8, n_demand = 4: 4, 16, 19, 34,

4, route_cost = 5.8, n_demand = 1: 14,

======Pickup time deviation is 88.43======================

Total cost: 293.220 (in Min)

==

1, route_cost = 184.3, n_demand = 24: 1, 2, 4, 6, 9, 10, 11, 12, 13, 14, 18, 19, 20, 22, 23, 25, 30, 31, 32, 34, 35, 36, 38, 39,

```
  2, route_cost =   74.0,n_demand = 10:   3,  7,  8, 16, 21, 24, 26, 33, 37, 40,
  3, route_cost =   18.8,n_demand =  3:   5, 15, 29,
  4, route_cost =   10.6,n_demand =  2:  17, 27,
  5, route_cost =    5.5,n_demand =  1:  28,


======Pickup time deviation is 94.70======================
Total cost:  286.633 (in Min)
============================================================
  1, route_cost = 189.7,n_demand = 26:   1,  5,  6,  7,  8,  9, 12, 14, 15, 18, 19, 21,
22, 24, 25, 27, 30, 31, 32, 33, 34, 35, 37, 38, 39, 40,
  2, route_cost =   71.5,n_demand = 10:   2,  4, 10, 13, 17, 20, 23, 26, 29, 36,
  3, route_cost =   25.5,n_demand =  4:   3, 11, 16, 28,


======Pickup time deviation is 107.63=====================
Total cost:  294.585 (in Min)
============================================================
  1, route_cost = 152.4,n_demand = 21:   1,  3,  4,  6,  7,  9, 12, 13, 14, 15, 16, 20,
21, 24, 25, 29, 32, 33, 35, 37, 39,
  2, route_cost =   95.8,n_demand = 13:   2,  5,  8, 10, 17, 19, 22, 23, 26, 30, 34, 36,
40,
  3, route_cost =   39.6,n_demand =  5:  11, 18, 28, 31, 38,
  4, route_cost =    6.9,n_demand =  1:  27,


======Pickup time deviation is 111.47=====================
Total cost:  292.093 (in Min)
============================================================
  1, route_cost = 137.8,n_demand = 19:   1,  3,  5,  6,  9, 10, 11, 14, 16, 18, 20, 25,
27, 29, 30, 32, 34, 37, 40,
  2, route_cost = 103.9,n_demand = 13:   2,  4,  8, 12, 15, 17, 22, 23, 28, 31, 33, 35,
39,
  3, route_cost =   34.4,n_demand =  6:   7, 13, 19, 21, 24, 36,
  4, route_cost =   16.0,n_demand =  2:  26, 38,


======Pickup time deviation is 123.90=====================
```

```
total cost:  300.392 (in Min)
==================================================================
  1, route_cost = 178.6,n_demand = 24:   1,  5,  8, 10, 12, 14, 15, 16, 18, 19, 20, 21,
22, 23, 24, 25, 26, 27, 28, 30, 35, 36, 38, 39,
  2, route_cost =  84.8,n_demand = 10:   2,  6,  9, 11, 13, 17, 29, 33, 37, 40,
  3, route_cost =  24.2,n_demand =  4:   3,  7, 31, 34,
  4, route_cost =  12.8,n_demand =  2:   4, 32,
```

Appendix F: Survey Questionnaire

Users' Views on Taxi Services in Singapore

We are students at the National University of Singapore, the survey conducted here is an attempt to explore the potential to improve taxi services currently in Singapore:

Get a taxi via street hail or at taxi stands --You pay what the meter shows only
Book a taxi to serve you immediately -- Extra Current-Booking fee around $ 3
Book a taxi in advance (at least 30 min earlier) -- Extra Advance-Booking fee around $ 5

We would like to investigate the above services with users like you. Your contribution is much appreciated.

***Gender*:** ☐ **Male** ☐ **Female**

***Age*:** ☐ **Under 20** ☐ **21-30** ☐ **31-40** ☐ **41-50** ☐ **50-60** ☐ **Over 60**

Family Income/Month (if you are single, choose your own income):

☐ **Under $ 2,000** ☐ **$ 2,000-4,000** ☐ **$ 4,000-6,000** ☐ **$ 6,000-8,000** ☐ **Over $ 8,000**

1. How often do you take taxi?

☐ Less than 2 per week ☐ 3-4 per week ☐ 5-6 per week ☐ 7 or more per week

2. How often do you use taxi-booking services?

☐ Never ☐ Occasionally ☐ 1-2 per week ☐ 3-4 per week ☐ 5 or more per week

(If you choose Never, please go to Question 5)

3. Why do you use taxi-booking services? (You may tick more than one)

☐ Brand loyalty

☐ Save time from queuing at taxi stand

☐ Cannot find taxi on roadside

☐ Guarantee to get a taxi at particular time

☐ Others (please specify) ____________________

4. If you book a taxi to arrive you immediately, usually where do you make the booking? (Please choose only one)

☐ At the pickup location

☐ On the way to the pickup location

☐ At office/home

☐ Others (please specify) ____________________

(If you choose "At office/home", please answer the following Questions a, b and c)

a. You usually book "At office/ home ", because

☐ You know the taxi will not arrive immediately (longer than 2 minutes)

☐ More convenient and comfortable to book at office/home

☐ Others (please specify) ____________________

b. Normally how many minutes do you book before the exact pickup time?

☐ Less than 5 minutes

☐ 5-10 minutes

☐ 10-15minutes

c. If the taxi can always arrive within 1-2 minutes or less than the walking time to the pickup location, will you consider changing your booking behavior?

☐ Yes, taxi arrival time should be the sooner the better; I will book it right at the pickup location.

☐ No, I would rather the taxi to arrive a bit later so I could book it at office/home.

☐ Others (please specify) ____________________

5. Currently, if you book a taxi more than 30 min in advance (Advance-Booking), you pay $5 booking fee, if you book less than 30 min (Current-Booking), you pay $3 booking fee.

a. If Advance-Booking fee is lower than Current-Booking fee, will you try to use Advance-Booking as much as possible?

☐ Yes

☐ No

☐ Others (please specify)______________________________

b. If Advance-Booking fee is free and taxi fare for Advance-Booking is even cheaper than street hail price, will you try to use Advance-Booking as much as possible?

☐ Yes

☐ No

☐ Others (please specify)______________________________

Do you have any suggestions to improve the taxi services in Singapore?

____

____

____

End of Survey

Thank You for Your Kindly Assistance.

Appendix G: Data of Respondents

Table G.1 Data of Respondents

NO.	Gender		Age						Income					Q1				Q2					Q3					Q4				4a			4b			4c			5a			5b		
	M	F	1	2	3	4	5	6	1	2	3	4	5	1	2	3	4	1	2	3	4	5	1	2	3	4	5	1	2	3	4	1	2	3	1	2	3	1	2	3	1	2	3	1	2	3
1		X				X						X					X					X		X	X	X				X		X	X				X		X		X			X		
2	X				X					X					X					X				X	X	X			X												X			X		
3	X				X					X					X					X				X	X	X			X												X			X		
4		X			X					X						X						X		X	X	X				X			X				X		X		X			X		
5		X			X						X					X				X				X	X	X			X												X			X		
6	X					X					X				X				X					X	X	X				X		X				X		X			X			X		
7	X					X					X				X				X					X	X	X				X		X				X		X			X			X		
8		X					X						X				X					X		X	X	X			X												X			X		
9	X			X					X					X					X						X	X				X		X			X			X			X			X		
10	X				X						X				X				X					X	X	X				X		X					X	X			X			X		
11		X					X						X				X					X		X	X	X			X												X			X		
12	X						X					X		X					X					X	X	X			X												X			X		
13	X						X					X		X					X					X	X	X			X												X			X		
14		X		X					X						X				X					X	X	X				X		X	X				X	X			X			X		
15		X		X						X							X			X				X	X	X				X		X				X			X		X			X		
16		X		X						X							X			X				X	X	X				X		X				X			X		X			X		
17	X				X						X				X				X					X	X	X				X		X					X	X			X			X		
18		X		X					X						X				X					X	X	X				X		X	X			X			X		X			X		
19		X		X					X						X				X					X	X	X				X		X	X				X	X			X			X		
20	X				X					X					X					X				X	X	X			X												X			X		
21		X				X						X					X					X		X	X	X				X		X	X				X		X		X			X		
22	X				X				X					X				X																							X			X		
23	X				X					X					X					X				X	X	X			X												X			X		
24		X		X						X							X			X				X	X	X				X		X				X			X		X			X		
25		X		X					X						X				X					X	X	X				X		X	X			X			X		X			X		
26	X			X					X					X					X						X	X				X		X			X			X			X			X		
27		X				X						X					X					X		X	X	X				X		X	X				X		X		X			X		
28	X				X					X					X					X				X	X	X			X												X			X		
29		X			X					X						X						X		X	X	X				X			X				X		X		X			X		

Table G. 1 (Continued)

NO.	Gender		Age						Income					Q1				Q2					Q3					Q4				4a			4b			4c			5a			5b		
	M	F	1	2	3	4	5	6	1	2	3	4	5	1	2	3	4	1	2	3	4	5	1	2	3	4	5	1	2	3	4	1	2	3	1	2	3	1	2	3	1	2	3	1	2	3
30		X		X						X							X			X				X	X	X				X		X				X			X		X			X		
31		X		X						X							X			X				X	X	X				X		X				X			X		X			X		
32	X					X					X				X				X					X	X	X				X		X				X		X			X			X		
33	X				X						X				X				X					X	X	X				X		X					X	X			X			X		
34		X		X						X							X			X				X	X	X				X		X				X			X		X			X		
35		X		X						X							X			X				X	X	X				X		X				X			X		X			X		
36	X				X						X				X				X					X	X	X				X		X					X	X			X			X		
37		X			X					X						X						X		X	X	X				X			X				X		X		X			X		
38		X			X						X					X				X				X	X	X			X												X			X		
39		X					X						X				X					X		X	X	X			X												X			X		
40		X			X					X						X						X		X	X	X				X			X				X		X		X			X		
41	X				X					X					X					X				X	X	X			X												X			X		
42		X		X					X						X				X					X	X	X				X		X	X			X			X		X			X		
43		X		X					X						X				X					X	X	X				X		X	X				X	X			X			X		
44		X				X						X					X					X		X	X	X				X		X	X				X		X		X			X		
45	X				X						X				X				X					X	X	X				X		X					X	X			X			X		
46		X		X					X						X				X					X	X	X				X		X	X			X			X		X			X		
47		X		X						X							X			X				X	X	X				X		X				X			X		X			X		
48		X			X					X						X						X		X	X	X				X			X				X		X		X			X		
49		X		X						X							X			X				X	X	X				X		X				X			X		X			X		
50		X		X						X							X			X				X	X	X				X		X				X			X		X			X		
51	X					X					X				X				X					X	X	X				X		X				X		X			X			X		
52		X		X						X							X			X				X	X	X				X		X				X			X		X			X		
53	X				X						X				X				X					X	X	X				X		X					X	X			X			X		
54	X			X					X					X					X						X	X				X		X			X			X			X			X		
55	X				X				X					X				X																							X			X		
56	X			X					X					X					X						X	X				X		X			X			X			X			X		
57		X			X						X			X				X																							X			X		
58	X				X					X					X			X																							X			X		

Table G. 1 (Continued)

NO.	Gender		Age						Income					Q1				Q2					Q3					Q4				4a			4b			4c			5a			5b		
	M	F	1	2	3	4	5	6	1	2	3	4	5	1	2	3	4	1	2	3	4	5	1	2	3	4	5	1	2	3	4	1	2	3	1	2	3	1	2	3	1	2	3	1	2	3
59	X				X					X					X					X				X	X	X			X												X			X		
60	X			X					X					X					X						X	X				X		X			X			X			X			X		
61	X			X					X					X					X						X	X				X		X			X			X			X			X		
62		X		X						X							X			X				X	X	X				X		X				X			X		X			X		
63		X		X						X							X			X				X	X	X				X		X				X			X		X			X		
64		X			X						X					X				X				X	X	X			X												X			X		
65		X			X					X						X						X		X	X	X				X			X				X		X		X			X		
66	X				X					X					X					X				X	X	X			X												X			X		
67	X			X					X					X					X						X	X				X		X			X			X			X			X		
68		X		X					X						X				X					X	X	X				X		X	X				X	X			X			X		
69	X					X					X				X				X					X	X	X				X		X				X		X			X			X		
70		X		X					X						X				X					X	X	X				X		X	X				X	X			X			X		
71		X			X					X						X						X		X	X	X				X			X				X		X		X			X		
72		X			X					X						X						X		X	X	X				X			X				X		X		X			X		
73	X						X					X		X					X					X	X	X			X												X			X		
74		X			X					X						X						X		X	X	X				X			X				X		X		X			X		
75		X			X					X						X						X		X	X	X				X			X				X		X		X			X		
76		X		X						X							X			X				X	X	X				X		X				X			X		X			X		
77		X		X					X						X				X					X	X	X				X		X	X			X			X		X			X		
78		X		X						X							X			X				X	X	X				X		X				X			X		X			X		
79		X		X					X						X				X					X	X	X				X		X	X				X	X			X			X		
80		X		X					X						X				X					X	X	X				X		X	X				X	X			X			X		
81		X				X						X					X					X		X	X	X				X		X	X				X		X		X			X		
82	X				X					X					X					X				X	X	X			X												X			X		
83		X				X						X					X					X		X	X	X				X		X	X				X		X		X			X		
84		X			X						X					X				X				X	X	X			X												X			X		
85	X				X					X					X					X				X	X	X			X												X			X		
86		X			X						X					X				X				X	X	X			X												X			X		
87		X		X					X						X				X					X	X	X				X		X	X			X			X		X			X		

Table G. 1 (Continued)

NO.	Gender		Age						Income					Q1				Q2					Q3					Q4				4a			4b			4c			5a			5b		
	M	F	1	2	3	4	5	6	1	2	3	4	5	1	2	3	4	1	2	3	4	5	1	2	3	4	5	1	2	3	4	1	2	3	1	2	3	1	2	3	1	2	3	1	2	3
88	X					X					X				X				X					X	X	X				X		X				X		X			X			X		
89		X			X					X						X						X		X	X	X				X			X				X		X		X			X		
90		X			X						X			X				X																							X			X		
91		X		X					X						X				X					X	X	X				X		X	X				X	X			X			X		
92	X					X					X				X				X					X	X	X				X		X				X		X			X			X		
93		X			X					X						X						X		X	X	X				X			X				X		X		X			X		
94	X				X					X					X					X				X	X	X			X												X			X		
95	X			X					X					X					X						X	X				X		X			X			X			X			X		
96	X			X					X					X					X						X	X				X		X			X			X			X			X		
97		X			X					X						X						X		X	X	X				X			X				X		X		X			X		
98	X			X					X					X					X						X	X				X		X			X			X			X			X		
99	X				X						X				X				X					X	X	X				X		X					X	X			X			X		
100		X		X					X						X				X					X	X	X				X		X	X			X			X		X			X		
101		X		X						X					X				X					X						X			X			X		X				X		X		
102		X		X						X					X				X						X	X				X		X			X			X			X			X		
103	X						X				X			X					X								X			X			X		X				X			X			X	
104	X			X					X					X					X					X						X			X				X		X		X			X		
105	X				X						X					X				X					X	X				X			X			X		X			X			X		
106		X				X				X							X	X																							X			X		
107	X				X					X				X				X																							X			X		
108	X				X					X				X							X					X				X			X				X		X		X			X		
109		X		X						X				X				X																							X			X		
110		X			X					X						X			X						X			X													X			X		
111	X							X					X		X				X						X					X			X		X			X				X		X		
112	X				X						X				X				X								X	X													X			X		
113	X					X			X					X					X					X						X			X				X	X			X			X		
114		X		X						X						X		X																							X			X		
115	X				X					X					X				X					X		X				X			X				X	X			X			X		
116		X		X					X					X				X																								X			X	

Table G. 1 (Continued)

NO.	Gender		Age						Income					Q1				Q2					Q3					Q4				4a			4b			4c			5a			5b		
	M	F	1	2	3	4	5	6	1	2	3	4	5	1	2	3	4	1	2	3	4	5	1	2	3	4	5	1	2	3	4	1	2	3	1	2	3	1	2	3	1	2	3	1	2	3
117		X		X									X		X					X				X						X			X		X			X			X			X		
118		X			X					X						X					X				X			X														X			X	
119		X		X									X			X				X					X			X															X	X		
120		X				X							X		X				X				X							X			X			X			X			X			X	
121		X			X							X					X		X					X				X													X			X		
122	X				X								X				X			X				X						X			X			X		X				X		X		
123	X				X					X					X					X				X						X			X			X			X		X			X		
124		X		X						X					X				X						X					X		X				X		X			X			X		
125	X			X					X								X		X					X				X				X									X			X		
126		X				X						X			X						X				X	X				X			X			X		X			X			X		
127		X				X					X			X					X							X				X			X			X		X			X			X		
128	X			X									X		X				X					X	X				X													X		X		
129	X			X						X				X				X																								X		X		
130	X			X						X				X				X																								X			X	
131		X			X						X			X				X																							X			X		
132		X		X						X				X					X						X	X				X		X			X			X			X			X		
133	X			X						X				X					X					X	X			X													X			X		
134		X			X								X			X				X			X			X				X		X			X			X				X		X		
135		X		X						X					X				X				X		X			X													X			X		
136		X			X						X				X				X						X					X			X			X		X			X			X		
137	X			X						X				X				X																								X		X		
138		X		X						X				X				X																									X	X		
139	X				X						X						X				X					X				X			X		X			X			X			X		
140	X						X				X			X				X																								X		X		
141		X		X						X					X				X						X			X													X			X		
142		X			X						X				X				X							X				X		X				X		X			X			X		
143	X			X						X				X					X							X				X		X				X		X				X			X	
144		X			X					X				X					X							X				X		X				X		X			X			X		
145		X				X				X					X			X																								X			X	

Table G. 1 (Continued)

NO.	Gender		Age						Income					Q1				Q2					Q3					Q4				4a			4b			4c			5a			5b		
	M	F	1	2	3	4	5	6	1	2	3	4	5	1	2	3	4	1	2	3	4	5	1	2	3	4	5	1	2	3	4	1	2	3	1	2	3	1	2	3	1	2	3	1	2	3
146		X				X				X				X					X						X			X													X			X		
147	X		X								X			X					X						X					X			X			X			X		X			X		
148		X			X								X	X					X						X				X												X			X		
149	X				X							X				X			X						X					X		X					X	X				X		X		
150		X			X								X	X				X																							X			X		
151	X			X						X						X				X				X	X					X			X			X		X			X			X		
152	X						X						X				X			X				X			X			X				X		X			X				X	X		
153		X		X						X						X			X							X				X		X				X		X			X			X		
154	X			X							X			X					X				X	X		X				X		X				X		X			X			X		
155		X			X						X				X					X				X	X	X				X			X			X		X				X		X		
156	X		X								X				X				X						X			X													X			X		
157		X				X						X		X				X																								X		X		
158		X		X						X					X			X																								X		X		
159		X			X						X			X				X																								X		X		
160	X			X						X					X				X						X			X													X			X		
161	X					X						X				X			X							X				X		X				X			X		X			X		
162	X			X					X					X					X						X	X				X			X			X				X	X			X		
163	X				X						X			X					X							X				X			X		X			X			X			X		
164		X				X						X			X			X																								X		X		
165	X		X						X					X				X																								X		X		
166	X				X							X					X			X						X				X		X					X			X	X			X		
167		X				X					X				X				X					X	X			X													X			X		
168		X		X					X					X					X					X	X			X													X			X		
169		X		X					X					X					X						X					X			X			X		X			X			X		
170	X				X							X			X				X					X	X			X													X			X		
171		X				X					X					X				X						X				X			X				X		X		X			X		
172		X			X						X				X				X					X	X	X				X		X				X		X			X			X		
173		X	X							X				X				X																								X		X		
174	X			X					X						X			X																								X		X		

Table G. 1 (Continued)

NO.	Gender		Age						Income					Q1				Q2					Q3					Q4				4a			4b			4c			5a			5b		
	M	F	1	2	3	4	5	6	1	2	3	4	5	1	2	3	4	1	2	3	4	5	1	2	3	4	5	1	2	3	4	1	2	3	1	2	3	1	2	3	1	2	3	1	2	3
175	X					X				X				X				X																								X		X		
176	X				X					X						X				X					X	X					X										X			X		
177		X			X					X						X			X					X				X		X			X			X		X			X			X		
178		X			X				X							X			X							X				X		X				X			X		X			X		
179		X			X				X					X					X								X			X			X		X				X		X			X		
180		X					X			X					X			X																							X			X		
181	X			X						X				X					X								X	X													X			X		
182		X		X						X					X				X					X	X					X			X		X			X			X			X		
183		X			X					X				X				X																							X			X		
184		X			X						X				X			X																								X		X		
185	X				X								X			X				X					X	X				X		X				X		X			X			X		
186		X				X			X					X					X							X				X			X			X		X			X			X		
187		X				X					X			X					X							X			X												X			X		
188		X	X						X					X				X																							X			X		
189	X			X							X					X					X				X			X													X			X		
190	X					X					X			X							X			X				X													X			X		
191		X			X						X			X				X																							X			X		
192		X		X					X					X					X						X					X		X				X		X				X		X		
193		X					X			X					X						X				X			X														X		X		
194	X			X						X				X					X					X	X					X			X		X			X			X			X		
195	X			X					X							X				X				X						X		X				X		X			X			X		
196	X			X							X			X					X							X				X			X			X			X		X			X		
197		X		X							X				X						X				X					X			X		X			X			X			X		
198		X		X						X				X					X						X			X													X			X		
199	X			X						X				X				X																							X			X		
200	X		X								X				X			X																							X			X		
201		X					X		X						X				X						X					X			X		X				X			X			X	
202		X			X								X		X				X					X				X														X			X	
203		X				X							X		X				X						X			X													X			X		

Table G. 1 (Continued)

NO.	Gender		Age						Income					Q1				Q2					Q3					Q4				4a			4b			4c			5a			5b		
	M	F	1	2	3	4	5	6	1	2	3	4	5	1	2	3	4	1	2	3	4	5	1	2	3	4	5	1	2	3	4	1	2	3	1	2	3	1	2	3	1	2	3	1	2	3
204	X			X						X							X			X					X			X														X		X		
205		X				X					X				X				X					X						X			X		X				X			X			X	
206		X		X						X					X			X																								X			X	
207		X			X								X				X					X		X				X														X		X		
208		X		X									X	X				X																								X			X	
209		X			X								X		X				X					X				X														X			X	
210		X				X							X		X				X						X			X													X			X		
211	X		X						X						X				X						X					X			X			X		X				X		X		
212	X			X						X						X			X					X				X													X			X		
213	X				X						X				X				X						X					X			X			X		X			X			X		
214	X				X						X						X				X					X		X													X			X		
215	X						X					X			X				X							X			X												X			X		
216		X			X						X						X	X																								X		X		
217	X				X					X					X				X						X			X														X		X		
218	X						X					X		X				X																								X			X	
219	X				X						X			X					X						X					X		X				X		X				X		X		
220		X		X									X		X				X					X				X													X			X		
221		X			X						X			X					X						X					X			X		X			X			X			X		
222		X			X						X						X					X	X	X	X					X			X			X		X			X			X		
223	X				X					X				X				X																							X			X		
224	X				X						X				X				X						X					X			X			X			X		X			X		
225		X				X						X			X				X				X							X			X			X		X			X				X	
226		X			X				X						X					X			X						X													X		X		
227		X		X						X				X					X						X					X			X			X		X			X			X		
228	X				X						X			X					X						X					X		X				X		X				X		X		
229		X		X									X		X				X					X				X													X			X		
230	X					X						X		X					X							X			X													X				X
231	X				X					X							X		X					X					X													X		X		
232		X					X					X					X		X					X				X													X			X		

Table G. 1 (Continued)

NO.	Gender		Age						Income					Q1				Q2					Q3					Q4				4a			4b			4c			5a			5b		
	M	F	1	2	3	4	5	6	1	2	3	4	5	1	2	3	4	1	2	3	4	5	1	2	3	4	5	1	2	3	4	1	2	3	1	2	3	1	2	3	1	2	3	1	2	3
233		X		X					X								X		X						X			X													X			X		
234		X			X						X					X					X			X						X			X			X			X			X		X		
235	X				X					X							X		X					X					X													X		X		
236		X					X					X					X		X					X				X													X			X		
237		X		X						X							X			X				X	X					X			X			X			X		X			X		
238		X		X						X						X				X					X					X		X				X		X			X			X		
239		X		X					X						X				X						X					X			X		X			X			X			X		
240		X			X				X						X			X																							X			X		
241	X			X						X				X				X																							X			X		
242	X				X						X				X				X					X					X												X			X		
243	X			X					X								X			X					X	X				X		X				X		X			X			X		
244	X				X					X							X		X					X					X													X		X		
245		X					X					X					X		X					X				X													X			X		
246		X		X					X								X		X						X			X													X			X		
247		X		X									X				X		X					X						X		X				X			X			X			X	
248		X		X							X						X					X			X				X													X		X		
249	X					X				X				X					X							X				X			X			X			X			X		X		
250	X				X					X							X		X					X					X													X		X		
251		X					X					X					X		X					X				X													X			X		
252	X			X						X					X			X																							X			X		
253	X				X						X			X						X						X			X												X				X	
254	X					X				X						X		X																								X			X	
255		X			X						X					X					X			X						X			X			X			X			X		X		
256	X				X					X							X		X					X					X													X		X		
257		X				X				X							X			X			X					X													X			X		
258		X			X							X					X			X				X						X		X				X			X		X			X		
259	X				X				X						X				X					X					X													X		X		
260		X					X						X				X				X				X					X			X		X				X		X			X		
261	X			X							X				X				X						X			X													X			X		

Table G. 1 (Continued)

NO.	Gender		Age						Income					Q1				Q2					Q3					Q4				4a			4b			4c			5a			5b		
	M	F	1	2	3	4	5	6	1	2	3	4	5	1	2	3	4	1	2	3	4	5	1	2	3	4	5	1	2	3	4	1	2	3	1	2	3	1	2	3	1	2	3	1	2	3
262	X				X					X					X			X																								X			X	
263	X			X					X					X					X					X	X			X													X			X		
264		X		X							X				X					X			X					X													X			X		
265		X		X									X		X				X					X				X													X			X		
266	X					X						X		X					X							X			X													X			X	
267	X				X					X							X		X					X					X													X		X		
268		X					X					X					X		X					X				X													X			X		
269		X		X					X								X		X						X			X													X			X		
270		X		X					X						X				X						X					X			X		X			X			X			X		
271		X			X				X						X			X																							X			X		
272	X			X					X					X				X																							X			X		
273		X			X				X					X				X																							X			X		
274		X	X							X							X		X					X				X													X			X		
275		X		X									X			X			X						X			X														X		X		
276	X						X				X				X				X				X			X				X			X				X		X		X			X		
277		X				X							X				X					X		X	X			X														X			X	
278	X			X								X		X				X																							X			X		
279		X	X									X		X				X																							X			X		
280	X				X					X					X					X				X				X														X		X		
281	X				X				X					X				X																								X		X		
282		X			X						X				X					X					X				X													X		X		
283		X				X				X						X			X					X				X														X		X		
284		X		X					X								X		X						X			X													X			X		
285		X		X					X						X				X						X					X			X		X			X			X			X		
286		X			X				X						X			X																							X			X		
287		X			X							X					X			X				X						X		X				X			X		X			X		
288	X				X					X					X			X																								X			X	
289	X			X					X					X					X					X	X			X													X			X		
290		X		X							X				X					X			X					X													X			X		

Table G. 1 (Continued)

NO.	Gender		Age						Income					Q1				Q2					Q3					Q4				4a			4b			4c			5a			5b		
	M	F	1	2	3	4	5	6	1	2	3	4	5	1	2	3	4	1	2	3	4	5	1	2	3	4	5	1	2	3	4	1	2	3	1	2	3	1	2	3	1	2	3	1	2	3
291		X		X									X		X				X					X				X													X			X		
292		X		X									X		X				X					X				X													X			X		
293	X					X						X		X					X							X			X													X			X	
294	X				X					X							X		X					X					X													X		X		
295		X				X				X							X			X			X					X													X			X		
296		X			X							X					X			X				X						X		X				X			X		X			X		
297	X				X				X						X				X					X					X													X		X		
298		X	X									X		X				X																							X			X		
299	X				X					X							X		X					X					X													X		X		
300		X					X					X					X		X					X				X													X			X		
301		X		X						X				X				X																							X			X		
302	X				X				X					X					X								X			X			X				X		X			X		X		
303		X	X						X					X				X																									X			X
304		X		X						X				X				X																							X			X		
305		X		X						X				X					X					X	X	X					X										X			X		
306		X	X						X					X				X																							X			X		
307		X		X						X				X					X					X	X	X			X												X			X		
308		X				X					X				X					X				X	X	X				X		X				X			X			X		X		
309		X		X					X						X				X					X	X	X			X												X			X		
310		X		X					X					X					X						X	X			X												X			X		
311	X		X						X					X					X						X					X					X			X			X			X		
312	X		X						X					X					X					X	X	X		X													X			X		
313		X		X					X					X					X				X		X	X					X										X			X		
314		X			X					X				X				X																							X			X		
315		X		X						X				X						X			X		X				X													X		X		
316	X		X						X						X				X						X			X													X			X		
317	X				X						X			X					X				X	X	X					X			X			X		X			X			X		
318		X		X					X					X				X																								X		X		
319		X		X					X						X				X					X	X	X			X													X		X		

Table G. 1 (Continued)

NO.	Gender		Age						Income					Q1				Q2					Q3					Q4				4a			4b			4c			5a			5b		
	M	F	1	2	3	4	5	6	1	2	3	4	5	1	2	3	4	1	2	3	4	5	1	2	3	4	5	1	2	3	4	1	2	3	1	2	3	1	2	3	1	2	3	1	2	3
320	X			X					X					X					X					X							X										X			X		
321		X	X						X					X				X																								X		X		
322		X				X					X			X					X					X		X				X			X			X		X			X			X		
323	X		X						X					X				X																							X			X		
324		X					X			X				X				X																									X			X
325		X			X				X						X					X				X	X	X			X													X			X	
326	X		X							X				X				X																							X			X		
327		X		X					X					X				X																									X			X
328		X		X						X					X					X					X	X			X												X			X		
329	X					X					X				X				X						X					X		X					X	X			X			X		
330	X			X						X					X				X					X					X												X			X		
331	X			X					X					X				X																								X		X		
332	X			X						X				X					X						X	X			X												X			X		
333	X					X							X	X				X																							X			X		
334	X				X					X					X				X						X	X					X											X		X		
335		X		X						X					X				X					X	X	X			X												X			X		
336	X		X							X					X				X					X		X				X			X			X			X		X			X		
337	X			X						X					X					X					X	X			X												X			X		
338		X	X						X					X				X																							X			X		
339	X		X						X					X					X						X				X														X			X
340		X		X						X					X					X				X					X														X			X
341	X			X					X					X					X						X	X				X			X				X		X		X			X		
342		X	X						X					X					X						X	X		X															X	X		
343		X	X						X					X				X																								X			X	
344	X				X					X				X						X				X	X						X										X			X		
345		X		X					X					X					X						X			X													X			X		
346	X				X				X					X				X																									X			X
347	X			X						X							X		X						X					X		X				X		X				X		X		
348	X			X					X					X					X						X																	X			X	

Table G. 1 (Continued)

NO.	Gender		Age						Income					Q1				Q2					Q3					Q4				4a			4b			4c			5a			5b		
	M	F	1	2	3	4	5	6	1	2	3	4	5	1	2	3	4	1	2	3	4	5	1	2	3	4	5	1	2	3	4	1	2	3	1	2	3	1	2	3	1	2	3	1	2	3
349		X			X					X				X					X					X	X				X													X			X	
350		X		X					X					X					X						X						X										X			X		
351		X		X						X							X			X							X	X													X			X		
352	X			X					X						X				X						X			X														X		X		
353		X		X					X						X				X								X				X										X			X		
354	X		X						X						X					X					X				X													X			X	
355	X			X						X				X					X					X	X	X		X													X			X		
356	X		X						X					X				X																								X		X		
357		X		X					X					X						X			X		X	X			X												X			X		
358	X				X				X						X			X																								X		X		
359		X		X						X				X				X																									X			X
360		X			X						X						X		X						X					X			X			X		X					X			X
361	X			X						X				X					X					X		X		X													X				X	
362		X			X				X							X		X																							X			X		
363	X			X					X					X					X																						X			X		
364	X				X				X					X				X																									X			X
365		X		X						X					X				X						X			X													X			X		
366		X		X					X					X					X						X						X										X			X		
367	X			X					X					X				X																							X			X		
368	X				X						X			X				X																								X		X		
369	X				X				X					X					X					X	X	X			X													X		X		
370	X				X					X				X					X						X	X			X													X		X		
371		X		X					X					X					X						X				X													X		X		
372	X			X						X				X					X								X				X												X	X		
373		X		X					X					X				X																								X		X		
374	X				X					X				X				X																								X		X		
375	X			X					X					X				X																								X		X		
376	X			X						X				X				X																								X		X		
377		X		X						X					X				X					X	X	X		X													X			X		

Table G. 1 (Continued)

NO.	Gender		Age						Income					Q1				Q2					Q3					Q4				4a			4b			4c			5a			5b		
	M	F	1	2	3	4	5	6	1	2	3	4	5	1	2	3	4	1	2	3	4	5	1	2	3	4	5	1	2	3	4	1	2	3	1	2	3	1	2	3	1	2	3	1	2	3
378		X	X						X					X				X																									X		X		
379	X		X							X				X					X						X				X												X			X		
380	X			X						X				X					X					X	X	X			X													X		X		
381		X	X						X					X				X																								X		X		
382		X				X			X						X				X						X	X			X													X			X	
383	X				X					X					X					X				X	X	X			X														X	X		
384		X		X					X					X					X						X				X													X		X		
385		X		X						X				X					X						X				X													X		X		
386	X				X						X			X					X					X	X	X		X														X		X		
387	X			X						X				X					X																								X	X		
388		X	X						X					X				X																								X		X		
389	X				X						X			X				X																								X		X		
390	X			X						X				X					X						X			X														X		X		
391		X					X				X			X					X					X					X													X		X		
392	X				X				X					X				X																								X		X		
393	X		X						X					X				X																								X			X	
394	X			X					X					X				X																								X		X		
395		X				X			X					X					X					X	X	X	X		X												X			X		
396		X		X						X				X				X																								X		X		
397		X			X					X					X					X				X	X	X				X			X		X			X			X			X		
398	X			X						X				X					X						X	X			X												X			X		
399		X	X						X					X					X						X				X												X			X		
400	X					X					X				X					X				X	X	X			X													X		X		
401	X			X						X				X					X						X	X			X												X			X		
402		X			X					X					X					X						X				X			X		X			X			X			X		
403		X		X					X					X					X						X			X													X			X		
404	X				X						X			X				X																								X			X	
405		X		X						X				X					X					X					X												X			X		
406	X			X					X					X				X																								X		X		

Table G. 1 (Continued)

NO.	Gender		Age						Income					Q1				Q2					Q3					Q4				4a			4b			4c			5a			5b		
	M	F	1	2	3	4	5	6	1	2	3	4	5	1	2	3	4	1	2	3	4	5	1	2	3	4	5	1	2	3	4	1	2	3	1	2	3	1	2	3	1	2	3	1	2	3
407	X			X						X					X					X					X	X				X			X			X		X			X			X		
408		X					X			X				X					X					X				X													X			X		
409	X			X						X						X			X						X			X													X			X		
410	X				X					X				X				X																								X		X		
411		X		X						X					X					X				X		X				X			X			X		X			X			X		
412	X			X						X				X					X					X				X													X			X		
413		X		X						X						X					X					X				X			X			X		X			X			X		
414		X		X					X						X				X					X					X												X			X		
415		X			X					X				X					X						X			X													X			X		
416	X			X							X				X						X					X				X			X				X		X		X			X		
417	X			X						X				X					X						X				X												X			X		
418	X		X						X					X					X						X			X													X			X		
419		X				X					X					X					X				X	X				X			X			X			X		X			X		
420		X		X						X					X					X					X	X			X												X			X		
421	X			X							X			X					X						X			X													X			X		
422		X			X					X				X					X						X			X													X			X		
423	X				X						X			X				X																								X		X		
424		X			X						X			X					X							X				X		X				X		X			X			X		
425		X		X								X			X				X						X					X			X			X		X			X			X		
426	X		X							X				X					X							X		X													X			X		
427	X		X						X					X					X						X			X													X			X		
428		X	X						X					X					X						X			X													X			X		
429	X				X					X				X					X						X	X			X												X			X		
430		X		X						X					X					X						X				X			X				X		X		X			X		
431	X				X					X					X						X					X				X			X				X	X			X			X		
432		X				X				X				X					X						X			X														X		X		
433		X		X					X					X					X						X				X												X			X		
434		X		X							X					X						X				X				X			X			X		X			X			X		
435		X			X					X				X					X						X			X													X			X		

Table G. 1 (Continued)

NO.	Gender		Age						Income					Q1				Q2					Q3					Q4				4a			4b			4c			5a			5b		
	M	F	1	2	3	4	5	6	1	2	3	4	5	1	2	3	4	1	2	3	4	5	1	2	3	4	5	1	2	3	4	1	2	3	1	2	3	1	2	3	1	2	3	1	2	3
436		X		X						X				X				X																								X		X		
437	X		X						X					X					X					X				X													X			X		
438		X			X					X				X					X						X			X													X			X		
439		X	X						X					X				X																								X		X		
440	X			X						X				X					X						X				X												X			X		
441	X			X						X					X					X						X			X												X			X		
442		X		X					X					X				X																								X		X		
443		X		X					X					X					X						X				X												X			X		
444		X			X					X						X						X				X				X			X			X			X		X			X		
445		X		X						X					X						X					X				X			X			X		X			X			X		
446		X					X				X			X				X																								X		X		
447		X		X						X				X					X						X			X													X			X		
448	X			X							X			X					X							X			X												X			X		
449		X		X						X				X					X							X			X												X			X		
450		X		X								X			X					X						X				X			X			X			X		X			X		
451	X			X						X				X				X																							X			X		
452		X			X					X				X					X						X	X		X													X			X		
453		X		X						X					X					X					X	X				X			X				X	X			X			X		
454		X			X						X			X					X					X		X		X													X			X		
455	X				X							X		X					X						X																X			X		
456	X			X						X				X					X						X			X													X			X		
457		X		X					X					X					X						X	X															X			X		
458		X	X						X					X				X																								X		X		
459		X		X								X		X					X						X																X			X		
460		X	X						X					X				X																								X				X
461		X		X					X					X					X					X	X			X													X			X		
462		X		X						X				X					X																							X		X		
463		X			X					X					X				X							X				X			X		X			X			X			X		
464		X		X					X						X			X																							X			X		

Table G. 1(Continued)

NO.	Gender		Age						Income					Q1				Q2					Q3					Q4				4a			4b			4c			5a			5b		
	M	F	1	2	3	4	5	6	1	2	3	4	5	1	2	3	4	1	2	3	4	5	1	2	3	4	5	1	2	3	4	1	2	3	1	2	3	1	2	3	1	2	3	1	2	3
465		X		X							X			X				X																							X			X		
466	X			X					X					X				X																								X		X		
467		X			X						X			X					X						X			X													X			X		
468	X			X						X				X					X					X					X												X			X		
469	X			X						X					X						X					X				X		X				X		X			X			X		
470	X				X						X			X					X							X															X			X		
471		X		X						X					X					X					X	X				X			X			X		X			X			X		
472		X	X						X					X				X																								X		X		
473		X		X						X				X				X																								X			X	
474		X					X				X				X						X					X				X			X			X			X		X			X		
475	X			X						X				X					X					X				X													X			X		
476		X		X						X					X					X					X			X													X			X		
477		X			X					X					X						X				X	X				X			X				X	X			X			X		
478		X			X						X			X					X						X			X													X			X		
479	X				X						X			X					X							X		X													X			X		
480		X		X							X						X					X				X				X			X			X		X			X			X		
481		X			X					X						X				X					X				X												X			X		
482	X					X						X		X				X																								X		X		
483	X			X						X				X					X						X			X													X			X		
484		X		X						X				X				X																								X		X		
485		X		X							X					X			X							X				X			X			X			X		X			X		
486	X				X						X			X					X						X	X			X												X			X		
487		X		X					X					X				X																								X		X		
488		X			X						X			X					X					X				X													X			X		
489	X			X						X					X					X					X			X													X			X		
490		X			X					X				X					X						X			X													X			X		
491		X		X							X				X						X					X				X			X				X		X		X			X		
492		X			X						X			X					X						X			X														X		X		
493		X			X							X			X						X					X				X		X				X		X			X			X		

Table G. 1 (Continued)

NO.	Gender		Age						Income					Q1				Q2					Q3					Q4				4a			4b			4c			5a			5b		
	M	F	1	2	3	4	5	6	1	2	3	4	5	1	2	3	4	1	2	3	4	5	1	2	3	4	5	1	2	3	4	1	2	3	1	2	3	1	2	3	1	2	3	1	2	3
494		X				X					X			X					X						X	X			X												X			X		
495		X				X					X			X					X						X			X													X			X		
496		X		X						X				X				X																							X			X		
497	X				X						X				X				X							X			X												X			X		
498	X			X						X					X				X						X	X			X												X			X		
499		X			X						X				X				X						X					X			X			X		X			X			X		
500		X		X					X					X					X					X				X													X			X		
501	X				X						X				X					X					X			X													X			X		
502		X		X					X					X				X																							X			X		
503		X			X						X				X					X					X	X				X			X			X			X		X			X		
504	X						X						X	X				X																							X			X		
505		X		X					X					X				X																							X			X		
506		X		X					X					X				X																							X			X		
507	X				X					X				X				X																								X		X		
508		X	X						X					X					X						X			X													X			X		
509		X			X					X						X				X					X					X			X			X		X			X			X		
510		X		X						X					X				X						X	X		X													X			X		
511		X		X					X						X				X						X			X													X			X		
512		X			X					X				X					X							X				X			X			X			X		X			X		
513	X				X						X				X				X						X			X													X			X		
514		X			X							X			X						X			X						X			X			X			X		X			X		
515	X			X						X				X					X						X	X				X			X			X			X		X			X		
516	X		X						X					X				X																							X			X		
517	X		X						X							X			X						X					X		X				X		X			X			X		
518		X				X			X					X				X																							X			X		
519	X			X							X				X				X						X			X													X			X		
520		X				X			X					X				X																							X			X		
521		X				X					X				X						X			X	X	X		X													X			X		
522	X			X					X					X					X						X			X													X			X		

Table G. 1 (Continued)

NO.	Gender		Age						Income					Q1				Q2					Q3					Q4				4a			4b			4c			5a			5b		
	M	F	1	2	3	4	5	6	1	2	3	4	5	1	2	3	4	1	2	3	4	5	1	2	3	4	5	1	2	3	4	1	2	3	1	2	3	1	2	3	1	2	3	1	2	3
523		X		X					X					X				X																							X			X		
524		X	X						X					X				X																							X			X		
525	X		X						X					X				X																							X			X		
526	X			X					X					X				X																							X			X		
527		X			X						X						X				X			X	X					X			X				X		X		X			X		
528		X				X						X				X				X					X	X		X													X			X		
529		X						X		X					X				X						X			X													X			X		
530	X			X					X					X					X						X			X													X			X		
531	X		X						X					X				X																							X			X		
532	X		X						X						X				X							X			X												X			X		
533	X		X						X					X					X						X					X			X			X			X		X			X		
534	X				X						X				X				X							X				X			X			X			X		X			X		
535	X				X					X				X				X																							X			X		
536	X			X					X					X				X																							X			X		
537		X		X					X					X				X																							X			X		
538		X		X						X					X				X						X	X		X													X			X		
539	X					X						X			X					X					X			X													X			X		
540		X			X						X				X					X					X	X				X			X			X			X		X			X		
541		X				X							X		X				X						X	X		X													X			X		
542	X					X							X	X					X								X			X			X		X				X		X			X		
543		X			X						X					X				X					X	X				X			X				X		X		X			X		
544	X			X					X					X				X																							X			X		
545	X			X							X					X			X							X				X		X					X	X			X			X		
546		X		X						X				X					X						X			X													X			X		
547	X			X						X					X				X					X	X				X												X			X		
548		X			X						X				X				X						X			X													X			X		
549		X			X					X				X					X							X				X			X			X			X		X			X		
550	X		X						X					X				X																							X			X		
551		X					X				X			X				X																							X			X		

Table G. 1 (Continued)

NO.	Gender		Age						Income					Q1				Q2					Q3					Q4				4a			4b			4c			5a			5b		
	M	F	1	2	3	4	5	6	1	2	3	4	5	1	2	3	4	1	2	3	4	5	1	2	3	4	5	1	2	3	4	1	2	3	1	2	3	1	2	3	1	2	3	1	2	3
552	X			X						X					X				X						X			X													X			X		
553	X			X					X					X					X					X	X			X													X			X		
554	X				X						X				X				X							X		X													X			X		
555		X	X						X					X				X																							X			X		
556	X			X						X					X				X						X			X													X			X		
557		X					X			X				X				X																							X			X		
558		X		X					X						X			X																							X			X		
559	X				X						X				X					X					X	X				X			X		X				X		X			X		
560	X		X						X					X				X																							X			X		
561		X		X					X					X					X						X			X													X			X		
562		X	X						X							X			X						X	X		X													X			X		
563	X				X							X					X					X		X	X					X			X		X				X		X			X		
564	X					X					X				X				X					X	X			X													X			X		
565		X	X						X					X					X					X	X	X		X													X			X		
566		X				X						X				X					X				X	X				X		X					X	X			X			X		
567	X					X						X		X					X							X		X													X			X		
568		X					X			X				X				X																							X			X		
569	X						X			X				X				X																							X			X		
570		X						X	X					X				X																							X			X		
571	X					X					X			X				X																							X			X		
572	X		X						X					X				X																							X			X		
573		X					X				X			X					X							X				X		X					X	X			X			X		
574	X			X							X				X			X																							X			X		
575		X		X						X					X				X							X				X			X			X		X			X			X		
576	X			X							X				X				X						X	X		X													X			X		
577	X		X						X						X			X																							X			X		
578	X			X						X					X				X						X					X			X				X		X		X			X		
579	X		X						X						X			X																							X			X		
580	X		X						X					X					X							X				X			X				X		X		X			X		

Table G. 1(Continued)

NO.	Gender		Age						Income					Q1				Q2					Q3					Q4				4a			4b			4c			5a			5b		
	M	F	1	2	3	4	5	6	1	2	3	4	5	1	2	3	4	1	2	3	4	5	1	2	3	4	5	1	2	3	4	1	2	3	1	2	3	1	2	3	1	2	3	1	2	3
581	X				X							X			X				X						X			X													X			X		
582	X		X						X						X						X		X																		X			X		
583		X			X						X						X					X			X					X		X				X		X			X			X		
584		X		X						X				X					X							X				X			X			X			X		X			X		
585		X		X					X						X				X						X			X													X			X		
586		X	X						X					X				X																							X			X		
587	X		X						X					X					X							X				X			X			X			X		X			X		
588		X	X						X						X				X						X	X				X			X		X			X			X			X		
589		X	X							X				X					X						X			X													X			X		
590	X			X						X					X					X				X	X					X		X			X			X			X			X		
591		X		X						X				X				X																							X			X		
592		X			X							X			X				X						X			X													X			X		
593	X				X							X					X					X		X	X					X			X		X				X		X			X		
594		X		X						X				X						X				X			X			X			X		X					X	X			X		
595	X			X					X					X				X																							X			X		
596		X					X		X					X				X																							X			X		
597	X			X						X				X					X						X	X		X													X			X		
598		X			X						X						X					X			X					X			X			X			X		X			X		
599		X					X			X				X				X																									X	X		
600	X			X					X					X					X						X			X													X			X		
Sum	263	337	62	249	186	65	35	3	176	218	123	50	33	275	193	57	75	143	302	95	27	33	17	200	307	230	12	133	94	212	10	98	134	1	40	114	58	112	97	3	452	131	17	556	34	10
%																												29.6	20.9	49.2		42.1	57.5		18.9	53.8		52.8	45.8		75.3			92.7		
	600		600						600					600				600										449				233			212			212			600			600		
NO.	M	F	1	2	3	4	5	6	1	2	3	4	5	1	2	3	4	1	2	3	4	5	1	2	3	4	5	1	2	3	4	1	2	3	1	2	3	1	2	3	1	2	3	1	2	3
	Gender		Age						Income					Q1				Q2					Q3					Q4				4a			4b			4c			5a			5b		

Appendix H: Abstract of Recent Research Accomplishments

1. Wang, H., D. H. Lee and R. L. Cheu, Dynamic Routing Decisions for Commercial Vehicles Using Real-Time Traffic Information, Transportation Research Record (TRR), Journal of the Transportation Research Board 1882, 2004: 201-209. (SCI)
2. Lee, D. H., H. Wang, R. L. Cheu and S. H. Teo, A Taxi Dispatch System Based on Current Demands and Real-Time Traffic Conditions, Transportation Research Record (TRR), Journal of the Transportation Research Board 1882, 2004: 193-200. (SCI)
3. Wang, H., R. L. Cheu and D. H. Lee, An En-Route Security Monitoring System for Commercial Vehicles, Proceedings of The IEEE 6th International Conference on Intelligent Transportation Systems, in CD-ROM, Shanghai, China, Oct 12-15, 2003. (SCI)
4. Wang, H., D. H. Lee and R. L. Cheu, Diversion Strategies for Commercial Vehicle Using Real-Time and Future Traffic Information, Proceedings of the 2010 International Conference of Logistics Engineering and Management (ICLEM2010), 2010, 387: 925-933. (EI)
5. Wang, H., D. H. Lee and R. L. Cheu, PDPTW based Taxi Dispatch Modeling for Booking Service, Proceedings of The 5th International Conference on Natural Computation (ICNC'09), 2009: 242 - 247. (EI)
6. Wang, H., R. L. Cheu and D. H. Lee, En-Route Security Monitoring based on an Incident Detection Algorithm for Commercial Vehicles, Proceedings of The 6th International Conference on Fuzzy Systems and Knowledge Discovery (FSKD'09), 2009: 276-281. (EI)
7. Wang, H., R. L. Cheu and D. H. Lee, Logistical inventory approach in forecasting and relocating share-use vehicles, Proceedings of 2nd International Conference on Advanced Computer Control (ICACC2010), 2010: 314-318. (EI)
8. Wang, H., R. L. Cheu and D. H. Lee, Dynamic Relocating Vehicle Resources

Using A Microscopic Traffic Simulation Model For Carsharing Services Proceedings of the Third International Joint Conference on Computational Sciences and Optimization (CSO 2010), 2010: 108-111. (EI)

9. Wang, H. , D. H. Lee and R. L. Cheu, Dispatch Systems for GPS-Based Taxi Booking Services in Singapore, Proceedings of The 8th International Conference on Applications of Advanced Technologies in Transportation Engineering, 2004: 125-130. (EI)
10. Cheu, R. L. , H. Wang and D. H. Lee, Incorporating Telemetry and Car-Following Data for Real-Time Monitoring of Container Trucks, Proceedings of The 8th International Conference on Applications of Advanced Technologies in Transportation Engineering, 2004: 88-93. (EI)
11. Wang, H. and X. Qin, A study of the automated logistics system of YOUNGOR's distribution center, Proceedings of the 2010 2nd Pacific-Asia Conference on Circuits, Communications and System, PACCS 2010, 2010, 2: 194-197. (EI)
12. Wang, H. and W. Liu, A study of the integrated transportation and logistics information platform of Yangtze River Delta, Proceedings of the 2010 2nd Pacific-Asia Conference on Circuits, Communications and System, PACCS 2010, 2010, 2: 190-193. (EI)